ACCESS
Student Study Guide

Lessons 1–31

5341 Industrial Oaks Blvd.
Austin, Texas 78735

C
.84
PRO
1988
Dr. 8-10
Study Gde

5341 Industrial Oaks Boulevard
Austin, Texas 78735

10 9 8 7 6 5 4 3 2 1   88 89 90 91 92

CONTENTS

AREA I: PEER-RELATED SKILLS

Section A: Interpersonal Skills

Section B: Coping Skills

AREA II: ADULT-RELATED SKILLS

Lesson 17: Getting an Adult's Attention

Lesson 18: Disagreeing with Adults

Lesson 19: Responding to Requests from Parents, Teachers, and Employers

Lesson 20: Doing Quality Work

Lesson 21: Working Independently

Lesson 22: Developing Good Work Habits

Lesson 23: Following Classroom Rules

Lesson 24: Developing Good Study Habits

AREA III: SELF-RELATED SKILLS

Lesson 25: Taking Pride in Your Appearance

Lesson 26: Being Organized

Lesson 27: Using Self-Control

Lesson 28: Doing What You Agree to Do

Lesson 29: Accepting the Consequences of Your Actions

Lesson 30: Coping with Being Upset or Depressed

Lesson 31: Feeling Good About Yourself

LESSON 1. THE TRIPLE A STRATEGY

👉 **Important Points to Remember About the Triple A Strategy**

1. Assess

2. Amend

3. Act

⊟ **Negative Example A**

Narrator: Hank has missed the bus and needs a ride home. Brad's brother pulls up to give Brad a ride. Hank jumps in the car.

Hank: Lucky you guys came along. Give me a ride home, will you? It's not far from your house.

Brad's brother: (scowling) We're not going home right now, Hank.

⊞ **Positive Example A**

Narrator: The next day Hank misses his bus again. Brad is standing nearby waiting for his brother.

Hank: Hey, Brad. Do you think you and your brother could give me a ride home today? I'd really appreciate it.

Brad: It's fine with me. Let's see what my brother says. Here he comes now. (opening car door) Can we give Hank a ride home?

Brad's brother: Missed the bus again, huh, Hank? (He smiles.) Sure, hop in!

⊟ **Negative Example B**

Narrator: Kari sees her friend Deanne at a school dance. Deanne is wearing a bracelet Kari had never seen before.

Kari: Hi, Deanne. What an interesting bracelet. Let me see it! (Kari takes Deanne's arm and looks closely at the bracelet.) Where did you get this?

Deanne: (looking uncomfortable) In San Francisco.

Kari: Could you take it off so I can look at it?

Deanne: Uh, listen, I just remembered, I have to find Sara and ask her something. Bye. (hurrying away)

⊞ **Positive Example B**

Narrator: Kari is looking at Deanne's bracelet. Deanne is looking uncomfortable.

Kari: (to herself) Deanne looks uncomfortable. She's blushing, pulling her arm away from me, and looking around as if she hopes no one sees us. I guess I'm embarrassing her by looking at her bracelet. (letting go of Deanne's arm) Thanks for letting me look at your bracelet. What do you think of the decorations they made for the dance?

Deanne: (looking relieved) I think they're really great. Let's go take a better look at them.

Narrator: Both girls walk off together, smiling.

⊟ **Negative Example C**

Narrator: Angela is talking very seriously to Reba.

Angela: Reba, I'm your best friend and I think you should know some of your friends are getting mad at you.

Reba: (shocked) Why?

Angela: They think you're not a very good listener. It seems like whenever anyone has something important to talk to you about, like a problem or some exciting news, you're more interested in looking around to check out what's going on in the hall. Or, if we're talking to you on the phone, you forget things we've already explained. It's like you're not really listening.

Reba: (surprised) Thanks for telling me, Angela. I'll try to do better.

⊞ **Positive Example C**

Narrator: Reba and a group of friends are gathered by their lockers in school the next morning.

Sheila: Wait 'til you hear what happened to me last night!

Reba: (looking directly at Sheila) I can't wait to hear! What?

Sheila: (excitedly) Tony called me!!!

Reba: You're kidding! You've been interested in him for ages. What did he say?

Sheila: He asked me out!

Reba: Great! Where are you going?

Sheila: To a movie, I think. Who cares! I'm so happy about it. I couldn't wait to tell someone.

Reba: Well, I think it's really exciting. I can't wait to hear all about it after the date.

LESSON 2. LISTENING

Review of Lesson 1 (Triple A Strategy)

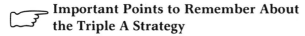 **Important Points to Remember About the Triple A Strategy**

1. Assess

2. Amend

3. Act

Lesson 2.   Listening

⊟ **Negative Example**

Narrator: Tara and Juanita are walking home after school.

Tara: Listen, Juanita, I think Lori is saying things about me to some of my friends.

Juanita: (looks across the street and waves to other kids) Oh yeah, what makes you think that?

Tara: (becomes intense) Well, last night one of my friends called and asked me a very strange question. She said that she had been talking to Lori.

Juanita: (still waving at friends) Oh Tara! You make such a big deal out of everything.

Tara: No, I don't!

Juanita: (steps off the curb and moves across the street) Hey, you guys!

Narrator: Tara stands on the curb looking hurt and worried.

⊞ **Positive Example**

Tara: Listen Juanita, I think Lori is saying things about me that aren't true.

Juanita: (looks at Tara) What makes you think that?

Tara: Karen called me last night and said that Lori told her that I stole my new coat from somebody's locker. It isn't true! I bought that coat with money I earned baby-sitting.

Juanita: What would make Lori think you stole your coat?

Tara: Probably because she's jealous. She always competes with me and gets mad if I have something she doesn't have.

Juanita: Do you think she was jealous about the coat?

Tara: Yes. But I earned it. I worked hard for it. So why is Lori telling people I steal things?

Juanita: I think you've already answered that question. What do you think you should do about it?

Narrator: Tara continues to tell Juanita her strategies for dealing with the rumors.

👉 **Important Points to Remember About Listening**

1. Maintain eye contact.

2. Let others do most of the talking.

3. Pay attention.

4. Avoid interruptions.

EXERCISE 1

Sheila: Wow, Kay. I notice you're wearing glasses. You've chosen some great frames. You really look great in them.

Kay: Do you think so, really? I feel different. I mean, sort of embarrassed. I was really getting hassled about not noticing people walking by because I just couldn't see who was waving at me.

Sheila: I know the feeling. I just got contacts last year.

Kay: I would've liked to have gotten contacts too, but I couldn't afford them. Glasses are hard to get used to. Now people don't recognize *me* for a change. (laughs)

Sheila: (laughing with Kay) Really, they do look nice. Kinda trendy too.

Kay: Well, thanks for letting me know. It makes me feel better. Nice to "SEE" you Sheila. (laughs)

✔ Checklist For Exercise 1

Did Sheila . . .   Yes   No

1. Maintain eye contact?   ☐   ☐

2. Let others do most of the talking?   ☐   ☐

3. Pay attention?   ☐   ☐

4. Avoid interruptions?   ☐   ☐

EXERCISE 2

Narrator: John has just quit work for the day, and Chris picks him up to go to a movie.

John: My boss is really bugging me these days. He wants too much. He keeps changing my hours. Tomorrow he wants me to work from 4 until 11 in the evening. I have studying to do, and he is always changing his mind.

Chris: (looking at John) You think your boss is asking too much of you?

John: Yeah, and he's critical, too. Every time I do something, it's not done right. Boy, I really hate my job sometimes.

Chris: What do you think you should do?

John: I could quit, but I need the money. The job really pays well for a high school kid, and it's not that demanding. It's just that my boss is too critical and changes my hours all the time. I just want things to be a little steadier. Maybe I could talk to him about it.

Chris: That's a good idea.

✔ Checklist For Exercise 2

Did Chris . . .   Yes   No

1. Maintain eye contact?   ☐   ☐

2. Let others do most of the talking?   ☐   ☐

3. Pay attention?   ☐   ☐

4. Avoid interruptions?   ☐   ☐

EXERCISE 3

Narrator: Mary and Karen are walking to another class after a test.

Mary: Boy! Did I blow that one.

Karen: (looking around and waving at friends) I thought it was easy.

Mary: I didn't know half the questions on that test. I've got to study harder. It was a terrible test.

Karen: You should have studied more. I started going over my notes last weekend and I re-read the chapter last night.

Mary: I got interrupted a lot last night, and one of the neighbors wanted me to baby-sit for an hour. It was a chance to earn a couple of bucks . . .

Karen: (interrupting) Well, you made your choice. You could have studied, but you decided making money was more important. So don't go around complaining about it now.

✔ Checklist For Exercise 3

Did Karen . . .   Yes   No

1. Maintain eye contact?   ☐   ☐

2. Let others do most of the talking?   ☐   ☐

3. Pay attention?   ☐   ☐

4. Avoid interruptions?   ☐   ☐

★ Situational Role Play Evaluation Guidelines

| | Situational Role Play | | | | |
	#1	#2	#3	#4	#5
1. Maintain eye contact.	—	—	—	—	—
2. Let others do most of the talking.	—	—	—	—	—
3. Pay attention.	—	—	—	—	—
4. Avoid interruptions.	—	—	—	—	—
Apply the Triple A Strategy	—	—	—	—	—

Lesson 2
Student Contract

Directions: Fill in the blanks with appropriate answers and check with the teacher.

When (under what circumstances) will you use the skill of listening?

_____

_____

_____

What might happen if you didn't use the skill of listening in the situation you described above?

_____

_____

_____

With whom will you use the skill of listening?

_____

_____

_____

What do you expect will happen when you use the skill of listening in the situation you described above?

_____

_____

_____

I agree to try the skill of listening with all its important points by (date) _____.

I will do my best to listen, and I will report back to my class accurately and truthfully about how I used the skill of listening and what the outcomes were.

_____   _____
Signed by student   Signed by teacher

LESSON 3. GREETING OTHER PEOPLE

Review of Lesson 2 (Listening)

☞ **Important Points to Remember About Listening**

1. Maintain eye contact.

2. Let others do most of the talking.

3. Pay attention.

4. Avoid interruptions.

Lesson 3. Greeting Other People

⊟ **Negative Example**

Narrator: Ted is shopping with his father in the mall. As they walk along, two boys pass them. Both boys wave at Ted and nod their heads. Ted keeps right on going without looking at them.

Dad: Ted, didn't you know those two boys? They seemed to know you.

Ted: Yeah. I know them from school.

Dad: Why didn't you say something or at least wave?

Ted: Ahh, Dad, it's no big deal.

⊞ **Positive Example**

Narrator: Ted is walking with his father in the mall. Two boys approach. Ted stops.

Ted: (waves to boys to come over) Hi, Juan. Hi, George.

George and Juan: (together) Hi, Ted.

Ted: Dad, this is George and Juan. Friends of mine from school.

Dad: Glad to meet you both.

George and Juan: (Each shakes hands with Mr. Smith.) Hi, Mr. Smith.

Ted: We're looking for a present for Mother's Day. What are you guys doing?

Juan: We were just checking out the record store.

George: But, now that you mention it, Mother's Day is coming up! I might just have to forget about buying

myself that record.

Juan: (laughs) You don't think she'd like your music?

George: Hardly, she hears enough of it as it is! But, if we're going to think of something, we'd better get moving.

Dad: Good luck! Hope to see you around again.

George and Juan: See you at school, Ted.

Ted: OK.

☞ **Important Points to Remember About Greeting Other People**

1. Look at and acknowledge the person.

2. Introduce others.

3. Show interest.

EXERCISE 1

Narrator: Rod is standing in line for a movie. He sees Julio, who is in his art class, approaching with a group of boys.

Rod: Hey, Julio.

Julio: Hi, Rod.

Rod: Checking out this movie?

Julio: Right.

Rod: (to the other boys) My name is Rod. I'm in Julio's art class.

Narrator: Julio's friends say hello to Rod and the boys begin a conversation.

✔ **Checklist For Exercise 1**

Did Rod . . .	Yes	No
1. Look at and acknowledge the person?	☐	☐
2. Introduce others?	☐	☐
3. Show interest?	☐	☐

EXERCISE 2

Narrator: Sandra is walking the hall at school with a girl she has just met. The girl has moved from another school. They meet Karen.

Sandra: Hi, Karen.

Karen: Hi, Sandra. Going to class?

Sandra: Yes. We're in a hurry but I'd like you to meet Sally. She's from Western High, but she's going to school here now.

Karen: Hi, Sally. Glad to meet you. Well, you guys get to your class. I'm in a hurry, too. I'll see you later, Sally.

✔ Checklist For Exercise 2

Did Sandra . . .	Yes	No
1. Look at and acknowledge her friends?	☐	☐
2. Introduce others?	☐	☐
3. Show interest?	☐	☐

EXERCISE 3

Narrator: Sally has moved across town to a new school. She has finally made a new group of friends and is attending a sports event with them. Her new school is playing her old school. She sees several of her old friends. They start to approach her and her new group, but she ignores them and goes right on talking with her new friends. Her old friends are surprised and disappointed.

✔ Checklist For Exercise 3

Did Sally . . .	Yes	No
1. Look at and acknowledge her friends?	☐	☐
2. Introduce others?	☐	☐
3. Show interest?	☐	☐

★ Situational Role Play Evaluation Guidelines

	Situational Role Play				
	#1	#2	#3	#4	#5
1. Look at and acknowledge the person.	—	—	—	—	—
2. Introduce others.	—	—	—	—	—
3. Show interest.	—	—	—	—	—
Apply the Triple A Strategy	—	—	—	—	—

Lesson 3
Student Contract

Directions: Fill in the blanks with appropriate answers and check with the teacher.

In what situation will you use the skill of greeting other people?

_____

_____

_____

What might happen if you didn't use the skill of greeting other people in the situation you described above?

_____

_____

_____

With whom will you use the skill of greeting other people?

_____

_____

_____

What do you expect will happen when you use the skill of greeting other people in the situation you described above?

_____

_____

_____

I agree to try to use the skill of greeting other people with all its important points by (date) _____ . I will do my best to greet other people, and I will report back to my class accurately and truthfully about how I used this skill and what the outcomes were.

_____   _____
Signed by student   Signed by teacher

LESSON 4. JOINING IN WITH OTHERS

Review of Lesson 3 (Greeting Other People)

☞ **Important Points to Remember About Greeting Other People**

1. Look at and acknowledge the person.

2. Introduce others.

3. Show interest.

Lesson 4. Joining In with Others

⊟ Negative Example

Narrator: Sonja and her family are at a picnic sponsored by her father's business. All the employees and their families are there. A group of people Sonja's age are gathered around the barbecue talking and playing a game. Sonja's mother urges her to join the group. She walks toward them, but hangs back. Finally, one member of the group notices her.

Girl: Hi, want to join us?

Sonja: I don't know . . .

Girl: Come on, we're having a good time.

Sonja: Uh, I don't have much to talk about. Anyway, I don't know the game you're playing.

Girl: Come over and watch. It's real easy to learn.

Sonja: Oh, I don't know . . . (She moves away from the group toward her family.)

⊞ Positive Example

Narrator: Sonja approaches the group confidently. As she comes close to the group, she waits for a break in the conversation and the activity.

Sonja: Hi, I'm Sonja.

Girl: Hello Sonja. I'm Jan and this is Hank, Joe, Karen, and Sue.

Sonja: What is this game you're playing? I think I'd like to try it.

Jan: Well, watch for a while and see if you want to join in.

Sonja: OK, thanks. (She watches and eventually joins the game.)

☞ **Important Points to Remember About Joining In with Others**

1. Find a person or group you would like to join.

2. Approach confidently.

3. Watch and wait for a good time to join.

4. Decide on the best way to join.

5. Join in and participate.

EXERCISE 1

Narrator: A group of students are making posters for a school play. Tim approaches the group, watches for a while, and waits for a break in the conversation.

Tim: Boy! You guys are really working hard.

Student: We have to get this done before the play starts next Saturday.

Tim: Need some help?

Student: Sure! Grab a brush.

Narrator: Tim joins in.

✔ Checklist For Exercise 1

Did Tim . . .	Yes	No
1. Find a person or group he would like to join?	☐	☐
2. Approach confidently?	☐	☐
3. Watch and wait for a good time to join?	☐	☐
4. Decide on the best way to join?	☐	☐
5. Join in and participate?	☐	☐

EXERCISE 2

Narrator: Chris sees a group of kids playing hackeysack on the front lawn of the school. He approaches the group and watches for a while. Suddenly Chris screams, jumps into the hackeysack group, kicks the hackeysack away from the group, and runs off. The group is very angry and one person chases after him.

✔ Checklist For Exercise 2

Did Chris . . .   Yes   No

1. Find a person or group he would like to join?   ☐   ☐

2. Approach confidently?   ☐   ☐

3. Watch and wait for a good time to join?   ☐   ☐

4. Decide on the best way to join?   ☐   ☐

5. Join in and participate?   ☐   ☐

EXERCISE 3

Narrator: A group of girls are talking near the stairs of the school. Linda approaches and, without waiting for a pause in the conversation, begins talking to one of the girls in a very loud voice. The rest of the girls look at her in disbelief. The group breaks up and Linda is left standing by herself.

✔ Checklist For Exercise 3

Did Linda . . .   Yes   No

1. Find a person or group she would like to join?   ☐   ☐

2. Approach confidently?   ☐   ☐

3. Wait and watch for a good time to join?   ☐   ☐

4. Decide on the best way to join?   ☐   ☐

5. Join in and participate?   ☐   ☐

★ Situational Role Play Evaluation Guidelines

	Situational Role Play				
	#1	#2	#3	#4	#5
1. Find a person or group you would like to join.	—	—	—	—	—
2. Approach confidently.	—	—	—	—	—
3. Wait and watch for a good time to join.	—	—	—	—	—
4. Decide on the best way to join.	—	—	—	—	—
5. Join in and participate.	—	—	—	—	—
Apply the Triple A Strategy	—	—	—	—	—

Lesson 4
Student Contract

Directions: Fill in the blanks with appropriate answers and check with the teacher.

When (under what circumstances) will you use the skill of joining in with others?

_____

_____

_____

With whom will you use the skill of joining in with others?

_____

_____

_____

What do you expect will happen when you use the skill of joining in with others in the situation you described above?

_____

_____

_____

What might happen if you didn't use the skill of joining in with others in the situation you described above?

_____

_____

_____

I agree to try to use the skill of joining in with others with all its important points by (date) _____ .

I will do my best to join in with others, and I will report back to my class accurately and truthfully about how I used this skill and what the outcomes were.

_____   _____
Signed by student   Signed by teacher

11

LESSON 5. HAVING CONVERSATIONS

Review of Lesson 4 (Joining In with Others)

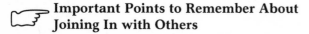 **Important Points to Remember About Joining In with Others**

1. Find a person or group you would like to join.

2. Approach confidently.

3. Watch and wait for a good time to join.

4. Decide on the best way to join.

5. Join in and participate.

Lesson 5. Having Conversations

⊟ Negative Example

Narrator: Julie is very excited about her new summer job. She sees Sue in the hall.

Julie: Guess what! I got the job I wanted this summer!

Sue: (with a grunt, looks distracted, is not enthusiastic) That's nice. What time is it?

Julie: Five minutes until class. I just wanted to tell you about it, Sue. It's such a neat job.

Sue: Well, I really have to go now, Julie. I'll see you later.

Julie: But I haven't told you about the job.

Sue: No big deal. You can tell me later.

⊞ Positive Example

Julie: Guess what. I got the job I wanted this summer!

Sue: That's just great! I'll bet you're really excited about it.

Julie: Yes, it's exactly what I wanted. It's going to be outdoors, the pay is pretty good, and I'm going to be with friends.

Sue: That sounds perfect. Tell me more about it.

Julie: Well, it's taking care of some lawns, and the girls that I'll be with are from West High. I know them all. We water and mow and prune shrubs. It's really great because we'll be out in the sun and we only have to work part of the day.

Sue: I'll bet the pay is good, too.

Julie: Yes, we'll get paid by the job.

Sue: You should make enough to have a great summer.

Julie: I just wish you could be with us.

Sue: Well, I've got my job at McDonald's.

Julie: Yeah, and that's a good job, too, because you can keep it all year.

Sue: We have to get to class, but you can tell me more about your job later.

Julie: OK!

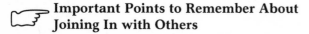 **Important Points to Remember About Having Conversations**

1. Listen about as much as you talk.

2. Show enthusiasm and interest.

3. Make sense; stay on the topic.

4. Keep the conversation going; ask and answer questions.

EXERCISE 1

Narrator: Wendy sees Gretchen coming down the hall.

Wendy: Gretchen! Just the person I've been wanting to see! Boy, did I want to tell you about the movie I saw last night! It was great and it had a terrific plot. There was lots of romance in it and everything. By the way, did I tell you about winning the 100-meter dash? I came in first over one of the best girls in the city. You should have seen it. I think I'll have a real good chance in the all-city girls' meet next time. Do you know what? I just heard that Jim broke up with Susan. I'll bet that Susan is really sad about that. You know I didn't get to tell you but . . .

Gretchen: (interrupting) Wendy!! You haven't let me get a word in edgeways.

Wendy: But I'm really excited about all this news.

Gretchen: Well, tell me one thing at a time.

✔ Checklist For Exercise 1

Did Wendy . . .   **Yes   No**

1. Listen about as much as she talked?   ☐   ☐

2. Show enthusiasm and interest?   ☐   ☐

3. Make sense; stay on the topic?   ☐   ☐

4. Keep the conversation going;
   ask and answer questions?   ☐   ☐

EXERCISE 2

Narrator: Brandon calls Dean on the phone.

Dean: (answering phone) Hi, Brandon.

Brandon: Dean, I just got a new adventure for a dungeon. We've got to play it.

Dean: What's it about?

Brandon: Well, I haven't really looked at it yet, but it really looks interesting. Maybe we could get the guys together over here tonight.

Dean: About what time?

Brandon: How about around 7:00?

Dean: That's fine, but I'm going to have to leave about 11:00. My parents are going hiking tomorrow and they want me to go with them.

Brandon: That's OK. We'll probably be through with it by 11:00.

Dean: I'm really glad you called. I'll bet John and Steve would like to play, too. Do you think it's a hard dungeon?

Brandon: Well, it looks pretty complicated, but we'll figure it out when we get together.

Dean: OK. I'll call John and Steve and see if they can make it.

Brandon: Great!! See you at 7:00.

✔ Checklist For Exercise 2

Did Brandon . . .   **Yes   No**

1. Listen about as much as he talked?   ☐   ☐

2. Show enthusiasm and interest?   ☐   ☐

3. Make sense; stay on the topic?   ☐   ☐

4. Keep the conversation going;
   ask and answer questions?   ☐   ☐

EXERCISE 3

Narrator: Ben, Jim, and Xavier have just finished playing a soccer game. Their team just barely won.

Xavier: Did you see that guy do that bicycle kick?

Jim: Yeah, that was great! I haven't seen anybody do that before, just like that.

Ben: We really stopped them in the last half. Our defense looks like it's going to work.

Jim: Yeah, our defense is looking better, but our offense needs some work.

Ben: Yeah, especially on the wings.

Xavier: Come on, you guys, the wings are doing fine.

Ben: Maybe we need to get the ball out to them better.

Xavier: That would help a lot.

Jim: I think the game was just great. We really took it to them.

Ben: We sure did. Xavier did a great job on the wing.

Xavier: Well, you guys gave me a lot of support.

✔ Checklist For Exercise 3

Did the boys . . .   **Yes   No**

1. Listen about as much as they talked?   ☐   ☐

2. Show enthusiasm and interest?   ☐   ☐

3. Make sense; stay on the topic?   ☐   ☐

4. Keep the conversation going;
   ask and answer questions?   ☐   ☐

★ **Situational Role Play
Evaluation Guidelines**

	Situational Role Play				
	#1	#2	#3	#4	#5
1. Listen about as much as you talk.	—	—	—	—	—
2. Show enthusiasm and interest.	—	—	—	—	—
3. Make sense; stay on the topic.	—	—	—	—	—
4. Keep the conversation going; ask and answer questions.	—	—	—	—	—
Apply the Triple A Strategy	—	—	—	—	—

Lesson 5
Student Contract

Directions: Fill in the blanks with appropriate answers and check with the teacher.

When (under what circumstances) will you use the skill of having conversations?

_____

_____

_____

With whom will you use the skill of having conversations?

_____

_____

_____

What do you expect will happen when you use the skill of having conversations in the situation you described above?

_____

_____

_____

What might happen if you didn't use the skill of having conversations in the situation you described above?

_____

_____

_____

I agree to try to use the skill of having conversations with all its important points by (date) _____ .

I will do my best to have good conversations, and I will report back to my class accurately and truthfully about how I used this skill and what the outcomes were.

_____   _____
Signed by student   Signed by teacher

LESSON 6. BORROWING

Review of Lesson 5 (Having Conversations)

☞ **Important Points to Remember About Having Conversations**

1. Listen about as much as you talk.

2. Show enthusiasm and interest.

3. Make sense; stay on the topic.

4. Keep the conversation going; ask and answer questions.

Lesson 6. Borrowing

□ **Negative Example**

Narrator: Sandy and Rachel share a locker. They meet there after lunch.

Sandy: What are you doing with my tape case? I've been looking all over for it because I wanted to listen to my new tapes at lunch.

Rachel: Oh, I saw it in the locker and borrowed it. I knew you wouldn't mind.

Sandy: Well, I do mind. I thought it had been stolen. I even turned in a report at the office. You ruined my whole lunch!

Rachel: But you always let me borrow your tapes before! I didn't think I had to ask.

Sandy: Well, I'm not going to let you borrow them again. Look! They're all mixed up and some of the labels are torn. Besides, when was the last time you loaned me anything? (Sandy walks off in a huff.)

⊞ **Positive Example**

Narrator: Rachel and Sandy are at their locker before lunch.

Rachel: Hi, Sandy. I was wondering if I could borrow your new tapes during lunch time today.

Sandy: Sorry, but I'm dying to listen to them myself. How about after school?

Rachel: Are you sure that's OK? I've been borrowing them a lot lately.

Sandy: Sure. It's OK. After all, you've let me borrow your tapes often enough. Besides, you always take real good care of them. I'll meet you here after school and give them to you.

Rachel: Thanks, Sandy.

☞ **Important Points to Remember About Borrowing**

1. Ask permission politely.

2. Don't become angry or disappointed when turned down.

3. Treat what you borrow as if it were your own.

4. If you borrow, be ready to lend.

EXERCISE 1

Narrator: Kelly sees his friend Mike at the park.

Kelly: Hey, Mike, let me use your bike to go over to the store and get something to drink.

Mike: Sorry, Kelly.

Kelly: Why not? I always let you use my soccer ball, don't I?

Mike: Yeah, but the last time I let you use my bike you left it unlocked and lying where a car could have easily run over it. My dad saw it and I got into trouble because of it.

Kelly: So, I'll lock it this time. Hand it over.

Mike: (riding away) Forget it, Kelly.

Kelly: (yelling after Mike) Some friend! Don't expect to use my soccer ball next time you want it.

✔ Checklist For Exercise 1

Did Kelly . . .   **Yes**   **No**

1. Ask permission politely? ☐ ☐

2. Not become angry or disappointed when he was turned down? ☐ ☐

3. Treat what he borrowed as if it were his own? ☐ ☐

4. Lend things of his own? ☐ ☐

EXERCISE 2

Narrator: Darla and her sister Leslie are getting ready for school.

Darla: May I please wear your blue sweater today?

Leslie: Yes. Please be careful with it, though.

Darla: Any complaints about anything I've borrowed from you?

Leslie: No. By the way, could I borrow your ski gloves this weekend?

Darla: Of course. You always borrow my gloves when you go skiing. It's a good thing we never go together. My hands would freeze.

✔ Checklist For Exercise 2

Did Darla . . .   **Yes**   **No**

1. Ask permission politely? ☐ ☐

2. Not become angry or disappointed when she was turned down? ☐ ☐

3. Treat what she borrowed as if it were her own? ☐ ☐

4. Lend things of her own? ☐ ☐

EXERCISE 3

Narrator: Lynn and Ginny are on the swim team. They are doing their workout when both stop at the wall between sets.

Lynn: I forgot to get a kickboard before I got in. Would it be all right if I used yours?

Ginny: I'm going to start the kicking drill set now, myself.

Lynn: That's okay. Serves me right for forgetting. Maybe if I have to get out and get a board enough times I'll learn to pick one up on my way in.

✔ Checklist For Exercise 3

Did Lynn . . .   **Yes**   **No**

1. Ask permission politely? ☐ ☐

2. Not become angry or disappointed when she was turned down? ☐ ☐

3. Treat what she borrowed as if it were her own? ☐ ☐

4. Lend things of her own? ☐ ☐

★ Situational Role Play Evaluation Guidelines

	Situational Role Play				
	#1	#2	#3	#4	#5
1. Ask permission politely.	—	—	—	—	—
2. Don't become angry or disappointed when turned down.	—	—	—	—	—
3. Treat what you borrowed as if it were your own.	—	—	—	—	—
4. If you borrow, be ready to lend.	—	—	—	—	—
Apply the Triple A Strategy	—	—	—	—	—

Lesson 6
Student Contract

Directions Fill in the blanks with appropriate answers and check with the teacher.

In what situation will you use the skill of borrowing?

_____

_____

_____

With whom will you use the skill of borrowing?

_____

_____

_____

What might happen if you didn't apply what you know about borrowing in the situation you described above?

_____

_____

_____

What do you expect will happen when you use the skill of borrowing in the situation you described above?

_____

_____

_____

I agree to try the skill of borrowing with all its important points by (date) _____
_____ . I will do my best to use the skill of borrowing, and I will report back to my class accurately and truthfully about my use of this skill and what the outcomes were.

_____   _____
Signed by student   Signed by teacher

LESSON 7. OFFERING ASSISTANCE

Review of Lesson 6 (Borrowing)

👉 **Important Points to Remember About Borrowing**

1. Ask permission politely.

2. Don't become angry or disappointed when turned down.

3. Treat what you borrow as if it were your own.

4. If you borrow, be ready to lend.

Lesson 7. Offering Assistance

⊟ **Negative Example**

Narrator: Rick hobbles out of Mrs. Lee's social studies class into the hall. He is on crutches and his leg is in a cast. He leans against the wall in the hallway and drops his books to the floor with a disgusted look on his face. His friend John walks up.

John: Boy! You really look mad.

Rick: Yeah, Mrs. Lee is really out of this world.

John: What do you mean?

Rick: Well, she won't give me extra time to do the assignment that's due next week.

John: Ha! So it goes, old buddy. I guess you win some and you lose some.

Rick: But I have this broken leg. I was out of school three days and I don't have notes for those days.

John: That doesn't make any difference to her because she knows she made the assignment before you broke your leg.

Rick: Yeah, that's what she said.

John: Well, see you later. (laughing) I guess this is not your day.

⊞ **Positive Example**

Narrator: Rick, hobbling out of the classroom on crutches, leans up against the wall and drops his books. John is coming down the hall.

John: You really look upset.

Rick: Yeah, Mrs. Lee is out of this world. She doesn't understand that I have a broken leg. She won't let me have any extra time on the assignment that is due next week.

John: Well, I know Mrs. Lee is not always the most understanding person in the world, but she probably feels its OK because she gave the assignment before you broke your leg.

Rick: Yeah, that's what she said, but I missed three days and I don't have the notes for those days.

John: Rick, I could lend you my notes for a while and maybe I could help you with your assignment. Would that help you out?

Rick: Sure, John, that would help me out a lot. At least you could tell me what went on in class during those days.

John: OK. I can meet you after school and we'll go over it.

Rick: I may be a little late because I'm not as fast as I used to be.

John: No problem. I'll wait for you in the library. Before I go, do you need help picking up your books?

Rick: Yeah, thanks.

👉 **Important Points to Remember About Offering Assistance**

1. Decide whether the person needs help.

2. Listen to what the person needs.

   Important points to remember for listening

   a. Maintain eye contact.

   b. Let others do most of the talking.

   c. Pay attention.

   d. Avoid interruptions.

3. Decide whether you can help or whether you know someone who can.

4. Offer to help and follow through.

EXERCISE 1

Narrator: Debbie is at her locker looking sad and worried. Katie, her locker partner, comes up and sees that Debbie has a problem.

Katie: Gee, Deb, what's the problem?

Debbie: Well, I don't know what to do. I'm going crazy! I'm so confused!

Katie: Calm down, Deb. Maybe if you told me about it I could help you with it.

Debbie: Well, about an hour ago Bob asked me to go to the Junior Prom with him. Bob's a really nice guy so I told him I would. But then just a few minutes ago Rick asked me to go to the Prom. Rick is my favorite person! You know how long I've wanted to go out with him? I just couldn't turn him down.

Katie: You mean you have two dates for the Prom?

Debbie: It looks like it.

Katie: What do you think you should do?

Debbie: Well, I really want to go with Rick, but Bob is such a nice guy and I don't want to hurt his feelings.

Katie: Which would make you feel worse, hurting Bob's feelings or missing a chance to go out with Rick?

Debbie: Boy, you really hit the nail on the head. When you put it that way I know exactly what I need to do.

✔ Checklist For Exercise 1

Did Katie . . .   **Yes**   **No**

1. Decide whether the person needed help?   ☐   ☐

2. Listen to what the person needed?   ☐   ☐

3. Decide whether she could help or whether she knew someone who could?   ☐   ☐

4. Offer to help and follow through?   ☐   ☐

EXERCISE 2

Narrator: As Tom walks down the hall he sees Kim trying to pick up several decorations and put them in boxes that have been tipped over.

Tom: Hi, Kim. What are you doing?

Kim: I'm trying to pick up these decorations. I've got to get them to the gym to decorate for the dance, and all the kids that were on the decorating committee have left.

Tom: Gee, Kim, that's too bad. Well, see you later.

✔ Checklist For Exercise 2

Did Tom . . .   **Yes**   **No**

1. Decide whether the person needed help?   ☐   ☐

2. Listen to what the person needed?   ☐   ☐

3. Decide whether he could help or whether he knew someone who could?   ☐   ☐

4. Offer to help and follow through?   ☐   ☐

EXERCISE 3

Narrator: Angela storms out of the house. Casey is there to pick her up to go to school.

Casey: What's wrong?

Angela: My folks grounded me for the whole week!

Casey: That's awful! Why?

Angela: Because I got in late last night.

Casey: What do you mean you got in late?

Angela: Well, you know what a junker Doug drives. It had a flat tire and we were late getting home. After 12.

Casey: But that wasn't your fault.

Angela: I know, but my folks won't listen.

Casey: Maybe if you can get them to listen, they will be fair about this.

Angela: My parents fair? That'll be the day!

Casey: I'll bet they'll be fair if you try to explain it to them calmly. Maybe if you tried to explain it to me on the way to school it would give you practice in explaining it to them later.

Angela: Hey, great idea! You tell me whether it sounds good or not.

Casey: OK, start at the beginning.

✔ Checklist For Exercise 3

Did Casey . . .   **Yes**   **No**

1. Decide whether the person needed help?   ☐   ☐

2. Listen to what the person needed?   ☐   ☐

3. Decide whether he could help or whether he knew someone who could?   ☐   ☐

4. Offer to help and follow through?   ☐   ☐

★ Situational Role Play Evaluation Guidelines

	Situational Role Play				
	#1	#2	#3	#4	#5
1. Decide whether the person needs help.	—	—	—	—	—
2. Listen to what the person needs.	—	—	—	—	—
3. Decide whether you can help or whether you know someone who can.	—	—	—	—	—
4. Offer to help and follow through.	—	—	—	—	—
Apply the Triple A Strategy	—	—	—	—	—

Lesson 7
Student Contract

Directions: Fill in the blanks with appropriate answers and check with the teacher.

In what situation could you use the skill of offering assistance?

_____

_____

_____

With whom will you use the skill of offering assistance?

_____

_____

_____

What do you expect will happen when you use the skill of offering assistance in the situation you described above?

_____

_____

_____

What might happen if you didn't use the skill of offering assistance in the situation you described above?

_____

_____

_____

I agree to try the skill of offering assistance with all its important points by (date) _____
_____ .

I will do my best to offer assistance, and I will report back to my class accurately and truthfully about how I used this skill and what the outcomes were.

_____   _____
Signed by student   Signed by teacher

LESSON 8. COMPLIMENTING

Review of Lesson 7 (Offering Assistance)

☞ **Important Points to Remember About Offering Assistance**

1. Decide whether the person needs help.

2. Listen to what the person needs.

3. Decide whether you can help or whether you know someone who can.

4. Offer to help and follow through.

Lesson 8. Complimenting

⊟ **Negative Example**

Narrator: Bart attends a large high school with a huge campus. Bart noticed that wheelchair-bound students were having difficulties getting themselves around in time for classes. He recently organized a league of students willing to assist wheelchair students who had requested or required help. A team of teachers named him outstanding student of the month at a student body assembly in recognition of his efforts.

Peter: Do you really think Bart should've gotten that award today? I think it was a lot of fluff and hype.

Craig: Peter, Bart made local headlines in the *City* paper! I think it's just great for Bart and the school, too.

Peter: (to himself) Oh no, here he comes now!

Bart: Hey guys!

Peter: Say, uh, Bart, you trying to run for mayor or something?

Bart: What do you mean, Pete?

Peter: That was some political move of yours, getting that club of, uh, "pushers" (laughs) started.

Bart: I don't know what you're saying, Peter. Why, you offered a lot of good ideas yourself, like advertising it in the school newspaper. Your being editor really helped out. I feel as if we should be sharing this award. Besides, I just heard that . . .

Peter: (interrupting) Well, you know, Bart, I'm not quite the teacher's pet you are, now am I? Gotta go! (to him-self) I've worked hard as newspaper editor, I should have gotten the award!

⊞ **Positive Example**

Peter: I think Bart really deserved that award today. He sure did a primo job of organizing that club. A great idea.

Craig: I do, too. It even made local headlines in the city paper!

Peter: (to himself) There's Bart. I'd sure like someone to say something to me if I had just won that award. (aloud) Hey, Bart! Way to go, buddy, congratulations on your award. We've just been standing here talking about the local headlines.

Bart: (Smiles) Hey, thanks for telling me that. And thanks for the advertisement boost. I don't think it could've happened without your help. I feel as if we should be sharing this award, but I've just heard you were nominated on next month's list.

Peter: No kidding? Again? Well, at least I won't have to worry about the competition next month.

Peter and Bart: (laugh, walk off to class together)

☞ **Important Points to Remember About Complimenting**

1. Recognize the value of a compliment.

2. Notice what you can compliment about others.

3. Express what you have noticed.

4. Be sincere.

EXERCISE 1

Narrator: Mave just started a new job as a bus girl. She's on her first training shift doing the best she can to watch and learn and still move fast enough for the head bus boy, Tyler, to be satisfied with her work.

Mave: Excuse me, Tyler, where can I find more ice?

Tyler: (impatiently) In the back, in the back, where else?

Mave: Uh, OK, I'll go look for it.

Tyler: Don't go running off for ice until you finish setting up the back tables.

Mave: I already did those.

Tyler: Oh, so you did; I didn't notice. Well, don't just stand there, go get some more ice!

✔ Checklist For Exercise 1

Was Tyler able to . . .   **Yes** **No**

1. Recognize the value of a compliment?   ☐ ☐

2. Notice what he could compliment about others?   ☐ ☐

3. Express what he had noticed?   ☐ ☐

4. Be sincere?   ☐ ☐

EXERCISE 2

Narrator: Beth, Sarah, and Jordan are standing in line talking together at fall registration, having just returned from summer vacation. Pat approaches the group from a distance.

Jordan: Will you take a look at Pat! She looks like half her old self. I bet she's lost 25 pounds. I hardly recognize her. Wow, you gotta hand it to her!

Beth: Used to hand it to her on a platter. (laughs) I wouldn't exactly say she's lost 25 pounds, would you? I don't think I like her hair that way at all.

Jordan: Come on, Beth, she looks great! I'm gonna say something to her. Anybody can tell that she's been trying really hard. Can't you ever think of something nice to say?

Pat: (approaches) Hello! Are we back to school already?

Jordan: Yeah, can you believe it? Pat, I was just saying to Beth how *great* you look! Tan, thin, new haircut. It's a new you!

Pat: Thanks, Jordan. Nice of you to notice. It wasn't easy. I'm still trying to lose some more, so I appreciate the encouragement.

Beth: Lose more? You gotta be kidding me. Trying to be glamorexia or something?

Pat: I'm sure I'm a long way from that. Well, I guess I better go hit the lines.

Jordan: Boy, Beth, that was a pretty backhanded compliment.

✔ Checklist A For Exercise 2

Did Jordan . . .   **Yes** **No**

1. Recognize the value of a compliment   ☐ ☐

2. Notice what he could compliment about others?   ☐ ☐

3. Express what he noticed?   ☐ ☐

4. Be sincere?   ☐ ☐

✔ Checklist B For Exercise 2

Did Beth . . .   **Yes** **No**

1. Recognize the value of a compliment?   ☐ ☐

2. Notice what she could compliment about others?   ☐ ☐

3. Express what she noticed?   ☐ ☐

4. Be sincere?   ☐ ☐

EXERCISE 3

Toni: Mrs. Leavitt, I just wanted to say thanks for sticking by me. I mean, I realize I haven't always been the best student or the easiest to get along with. Math has always been so difficult for me.

Mrs. Leavitt: Well, I have appreciated your effort. You stayed after school many times to work on assignments. Besides, I like it that you were never afraid to ask questions. It helped me be a better teacher.

Toni: And you've helped me learn how to study. I owe my grade improvements to you.

Mrs. Leavitt: I didn't do the work for you. Let's just say we learned a lot from each other.

✔ Checklist For Exercise 3

Did Toni and Mrs. Leavitt . . .   **Yes   No**

1. Recognize the value of a compliment?   ☐   ☐

2. Notice what they could compliment   ☐   ☐
   about others?

3. Express what they noticed?   ☐   ☐

4. Be sincere?   ☐   ☐

★ Situational Role Play Evaluation Guidelines

| | **Situational Role Play** | | | | |
	#1	**#2**	**#3**	**#4**	**#5**
1. Recognize the value of a compliment.	—	—	—	—	—
2. Notice what you can compliment about others.	—	—	—	—	—
3. Express what you have noticed.	—	—	—	—	—
4. Be sincere.	—	—	—	—	—
Apply the Triple A Strategy	—	—	—	—	—

Lesson 8
Student Contract

Directions: Fill in the blanks with appropriate answers and check with your teacher.

In what situation will you use the skill of complimenting?

_____

_____

_____

With whom will you use the skill of complimenting?

_____

_____

_____

What do you expect will happen when you use the skill of complimenting in the situation you have described above?

_____

_____

_____

What might happen if you didn't use the skill of complimenting in the situation you described above?

_____

_____

_____

I agree to try the skill of complimenting with all its important points by (date) _____
_____ . I will do my best to compliment, and will report back to my class accurately and truthfully about how I used this skill and what the outcomes were.

_____   _____
Signed by student   Signed by teacher

LESSON 9. SHOWING A SENSE OF HUMOR

Review of Lesson 8 (Complimenting)

☞ **Important Points to Remember About Complimenting**

1. Recognize the value of a compliment.

2. Notice what you can compliment about others.

3. Express what you have noticed.

4. Be sincere

Lesson 9. Showing a Sense of Humor

⊟ **Negative Example**

Narrator: Annette is trying out for the rally squad. It's the most important thing in her life at this moment and she feels she just HAS to make it. She has practiced for hours and hours. On the day of the tryouts she is very nervous, and when her name is called she nearly faints. As she begins her routine, she makes one blunder after another because she is so tense. Her routine is supposed to end up with her doing the splits. When she gets into the splits position, she can't get up. Two boys have to help her to her feet. By this time she is crying. She leaves tryouts early without finding out whether she made the squad.

⊞ **Positive Example**

Narrator: Annette is telling Sally about her experience in tryouts for the rally squad.

Annette: I went into it so seriously that I got all tense and couldn't perform the way I wanted to. I kept making mistakes and had to start over several times. But the funniest thing happened. At the end of my routine, I had to do the splits, and when I got down into the splits, I couldn't get up!

Sally: How embarrassing!

Annette: I'll say! It took two boys to get me up, and one of them fell over. It was so funny that everybody was laughing. I know that the tryouts were serious. I really wanted to make rally. But when that happened, there was nothing else to do but crack up.

Sally: Well, I'm glad you can laugh about it now. It makes it easier to take not making the rally squad.

Annette: Well, I'm sure I'll do better when I try out next time. At least everyone enjoyed my splits.

☞ **Important Points to Remember About Showing a Sense of Humor**

1. Have fun and enjoy yourself.

2. Try to find something funny in a difficult situation.

3. Be able to laugh at yourself.

4. Be able to take a joke.

5. Know when to show a sense of humor and when to be serious.

———————————

EXERCISE 1

Narrator: Karen and Shirley are practicing putting on make-up for a modeling class they are taking at one of the local department stores. Both girls are very serious about doing well in the class. Make-up is one of the important features of the class, and the girls have spent hours trying to get their make-up just right for the big modeling event. On this particular day they have spent about an hour and a half working on their make-up. Shirley has just started putting on her lipstick when the tube slips and spreads her lipstick across her cheek. Karen, looking at the mess on Shirley's face, begins to laugh. Shirley takes the tube of lipstick and spreads it across the other cheek. Laughing, both girls begin smearing make-up all over their faces and strutting around the room as if they were modeling. All the while, they are laughing and having a great time. Shirley's mother calls them to dinner. They begin cleaning up their mess.

✔ **Checklist For Exercise 1**

Did Karen and Shirley . . .   **Yes   No**

1. Have fun and enjoy themselves?   ☐   ☐

2. Try to find something funny in a difficult situation?   ☐   ☐

27

3. Laugh at themselves? ☐ ☐

4. Take a joke? ☐ ☐

5. Know when to show a sense of humor and when to be serious? ☐ ☐

EXERCISE 2

Narrator: Last night, in the championship basketball game, Kelly missed a free throw that would have tied the game and put her team into an overtime play-off. Because she missed, her team lost by one point. Kelly feels terrible about it. The next day in school, as she walks down the hall, kids make choking noises and call out comments like "Here comes the goat!" and "Hey, Kelly! Choke much?" At first Kelly wants to go home, but then she starts smiling and going along with the teasing. When people ask how she managed to miss a free throw, she puts her hands around her throat and makes choking noises. By the end of the day, kids are patting her on the back and saying, "We'll get them next year." Kelly's coach tells her she handled the situation well.

✔ Checklist For Exercise 2

Did Kelly . . .   Yes   No

1. Have fun and enjoy herself? ☐ ☐

2. Try to find something funny in a difficult situation? ☐ ☐

3. Laugh at herself? ☐ ☐

4. Take a joke? ☐ ☐

5. Know when to show a sense of humor and when to be serious? ☐ ☐

EXERCISE 3

Narrator: Anthony has a job at a fast food restaurant. One night, when it is very busy and the manager is in a bad mood, all the kids working at the restaurant are getting pretty tense and nervous. Anthony is working especially hard.

Anthony: Man, I'm whipping these burgers out so fast I'm getting McBlisters.

Leroy: Yeah, we know you're not used to working. Working HARD must be a real big event for you.

Anthony: Hey, better have the customers stand back a few yards from the counter. These burgers are moving faster than speeding bullets.

Narrator: Anthony and the other employees start to relax as they keep up the chatter. Even the manager and the customers pick up on their good mood.

✔ Checklist For Exercise 3

Did Anthony . . .   Yes   No

1. Have fun and enjoy himself? ☐ ☐

2. Try to find something funny in a difficult situation? ☐ ☐

3. Laugh at himself? ☐ ☐

4. Take a joke? ☐ ☐

5. Know when to show a sense of humor and when to be serious? ☐ ☐

★ Situational Role Play Evaluation Guidelines

	Situational Role Play				
	#1	#2	#3	#4	#5
1. Have fun and enjoy yourself.	—	—	—	—	—
2. Try to find something funny in a difficult situation.	—	—	—	—	—
3. Be able to laugh at yourself.	—	—	—	—	—
4. Be able to take a joke.	—	—	—	—	—
5. Know when to show a sense of humor and when to be serious.	—	—	—	—	—
Apply the Triple A Strategy	—	—	—	—	—

Lesson 9
Student Contract

Directions: Fill in the blanks with appropriate answers and check with the teacher.

In what situation will you use the skill of showing a sense of humor?

_____

_____

_____

What might happen if you didn't use the skill of showing a sense of humor in the situation you described above?

_____

_____

_____

With whom will you use the skill of showing a sense of humor?

_____

_____

_____

What do you expect will happen when you use the skill of showing a sense of humor in the situation you described above?

_____

_____

_____

I agree to try to use the skill of showing a sense of humor with all its important points by (date) _____ . I will do my best to show a sense of humor, and I will report back to my class accurately and truthfully about how I used this skill and what the outcomes were.

_____   _____
Signed by student   Signed by teacher

LESSON 10. KEEPING FRIENDS

Review of Lesson 9 (Showing a Sense of Humor)

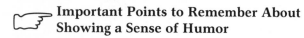 **Important Points to Remember About Showing a Sense of Humor**

1. Have fun and enjoy yourself.

2. Try to find something funny in a difficult situation.

3. Be able to laugh at yourself.

4. Be able to take a joke.

5. Know when to show a sense of humor and when to be serious.

Lesson 10. Keeping Friends

⊟ Negative Example

Narrator: Joan and Ann used to live in the same neighborhood and were good friends. Joan moved to a different part of town 2 years ago. Ann made several phone calls to Joan at first, but they were never returned. Now the girls haven't seen each other for a long time. One day they see each other at a shopping mall.

Ann: (approaching and waving) Joan, is that you?

Joan: Who else? I *always* shop here now. What are *you* doing here?

Ann: Oh, uh, I'm trying to get to the phone to call my mom to get a ride home.

Joan: I haven't thought about you for ages.

Ann: Well, it's been a long time since you left the neighborhood.

Joan: I see you haven't gotten any cuter.

Ann: (acting insulted) Gee, thanks for the compliment.

Joan: I have to be going now. I really have a lot of shopping to do.

⊞ Positive Example

Narrator: After Joan moved, she continued to call Ann and invite her to movies, parties, and other activities. Ann returned with invitations to outings with her family, sending birthday cards, and post cards. When Joan had a problem or was excited about something she would often call Ann and share it, as would Ann. Sometimes they would borrow each other's clothes and records or tapes. They remained good friends, even though they were no longer neighbors.

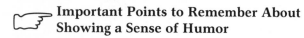 **Important Points to Remember About Keeping Friends**

1. Stay in contact.

2. Demonstrate thoughtfulness.

3. Be a good listener.

   Important points to remember about listening

   a. Maintain eye contact.

   b. Let others do most of the talking.

   c. Pay attention.

   d. Avoid interruptions.

4. Compliment your friend.

   Important points to remember about complimenting

   a. Recognize the value of a compliment.

   b. Notice what you can compliment about others.

   c. Express what you have noticed.

   d. Be sincere.

5. Offer assistance.

   Important points to remember about offering assistance

   a. Decide whether the person needs help.

   b. Listen to what the person needs.

   c. Decide whether you can help or whether you know someone who can.

   d. Offer to help and follow through.

6. Borrow the right way.

   Important points to remember about borrowing

   a. Ask permission politely.

   b. Don't become angry or disappointed when you are turned down.

   c. Treat what you borrow as if it were your own.

   d. If you borrow, be ready to lend.

EXERCISE 1

Wes: (calling Monte on the phone) Hi, Monte, this is Wes.

Monte: Hi, Wes.

Wes: I'm giving an end-of-the-school-year party and I wanted to make sure you could come before I call anyone else. It's a week from Saturday. Can you make it?

Monte: Sure, sounds great.

Wes: Well, it wouldn't be a party if you couldn't be there.

Monte: Thanks. Should I bring anything?

Wes: No, just yourself and a date if you want to.

Monte: Are you sure you don't need anything, like chips or tapes or something?

Wes: Well, sure, bring chips. That would be great. I haven't gotten any new tapes lately. If you have some new ones, it would be great if we could use them at the party.

Monte: I have a couple of new ones I'll bring.

Wes: I'd appreciate it, Monte. Well, see you at the party.

Monte: Yeah, thanks for calling!

✔ Checklist For Exercise 1

Did Wes and Monte . . .	Yes	No
1. Maintain contact?	☐	☐
2. Demonstrate thoughtfulness?	☐	☐
3. Show they were good listeners?	☐	☐
4. Compliment?	☐	☐
5. Offer assistance?	☐	☐
6. Borrow the right way?	☐	☐

EXERCISE 2

Narrator: Renée, and Beth had been on the girls' basketball team, but this year Renée is not playing. She still goes to all the games and congratulates Beth every time they win. The team is moving toward the state finals and Beth's team loses an important game. After the game, Renée goes to the locker room where she finds Beth crying.

Renée: (putting her arm around Beth) That was a hard one to lose, wasn't it?

Beth: Yeah, I feel miserable. We just needed two more baskets.

Renée: You had a good game, though. You played great, Beth.

Beth: Not well enough, I guess.

Renée: Hey, there were four other people on the floor with you the whole time. You can't take the responsibility for the whole game.

Beth: You know, I didn't think of it that way. Hey, thanks for coming, Renée. You're a good friend.

✔ Checklist For Exercise 2

Did Renée . . .	Yes	No
1. Maintain contact?	☐	☐
2. Demonstrate thoughtfulness?	☐	☐
3. Show she was a good listener?	☐	☐
4. Compliment her friend?	☐	☐
5. Offer assistance?	☐	☐
6. Borrow the right way?	☐	☐

EXERCISE 3

Narrator: Brandon has just been paid and can't wait to go with a friend to spend some of his money. He decides to go with Pete, but instead of calling Pete and asking him if he wants to go shopping, Brandon drives over to Pete's house. Pete is mowing the lawn as Brandon drives up.

Brandon: Hey, Pete, I just got paid and I want to spend it. Want to come along?

Pete: I'd like to, but right now I have to finish mowing this lawn.

Brandon: Oh, do it later.

Pete: No, if I don't get it done my dad will be mad and I may not get all of my allowance and . . .

Brandon: (interrupts) Come on, be a buddy and go with me. This job can wait.

Pete: Look, Brandon. I really have to get this job done. If you'd help me we could get it done faster.

Brandon: No way! I just got off work. I'm going shopping. See you later.

✔ Checklist For Exercise 3

Did Brandon . . .   **Yes   No**

1. Maintain contact?   ☐   ☐

2. Demonstrate thoughtfulness?   ☐   ☐

3. Show he was a good listener?   ☐   ☐

4. Compliment his friend?   ☐   ☐

5. Offer assistance?   ☐ ☐

6. Borrow the right way?   ☐ ☐

★ Situational Role Play Evaluation Guidelines

	Situational Role Play				
	#1	**#2**	**#3**	**#4**	**#5**
1. Maintain contact.	—	—	—	—	—
2. Demonstrate thoughtfulness.	—	—	—	—	—
3. Be a good listener.	—	—	—	—	—
4. Compliment your friends.	—	—	—	—	—
5. Offer assistance.	—	—	—	—	—
6. Borrow the right way.	—	—	—	—	—
Apply the Triple A Strategy	—	—	—	—	—

Lesson 10
Student Contract

Directions: Fill in the blanks with appropriate answers and check with the teacher.

With whom will you use the skill of keeping friends?

_____

_____

_____

When (under what circumstances) will you use the skill of keeping friends?

_____

_____

_____

What do you expect will happen when you use the skill of keeping friends in the situation you described above?

_____

_____

_____

What might happen if you didn't use the skill of keeping friends in the situation you described above?

_____

_____

_____

I agree to try the skill of keeping friends with all its important points by (date) _____
_____ .

I will do my best to keep friends, and I will report back to my class accurately and truthfully about how I used this skill and what the outcomes were.

_____   _____
Signed by student   Signed by teacher

LESSON 11. INTERACTING WITH THE OPPOSITE SEX

Review of Lesson 10 (Keeping Friends)

 **Important Points to Remember About Keeping Friends**

1. Maintain contact.

2. Demonstrate thoughtfulness.

3. Be a good listener.

4. Compliment your friend.

5. Offer assistance.

6. Borrow the right way.

Lesson 11. Interacting with the Opposite Sex

□ **Negative Example**

Narrator: Brad is on a picnic with a group of boys and girls his age. Brad knew Ginny would be at the picnic and he's been thinking for days that this is his chance to make an impression and get to know her. He's been thinking about the picnic so much that he's made himself nervous, and when he sees Ginny, he almost wants to avoid her. He's so afraid he's going to embarrass himself that, for a little while, he just doesn't do anything.

Finally, when the group starts to choose teams for a softball game, Brad approaches hesitantly. He hangs around the edge of the group and doesn't join in as everyone is teasing and laughing about how to make up the teams. During the game, he wants to do something that Ginny will notice, but he's so nervous he makes one mistake after another. When the other kids tease him about making dumb plays and dropping the ball, he blushes and feels even worse.

By the time the game is over, Brad is thinking he'll have to do something outrageous to get Ginny to notice him. There's a big pile of leaves and grass clippings in the park and several of the kids start throwing handfuls of the stuff at each other. Brad grabs a handful of leaves, rushes over to Ginny, and stuffs it down the neck of her sweatshirt. Ginny is startled and the leaves are dirty and scratchy. Brad runs off leaving Ginny annoyed and confused.

Some of the kids start swinging on the swings. Brad gets going very high, yelling at everyone to watch. When the swing is at the highest point he suddenly jumps out. As he comes down he hears his ankle snap and pain shoots up his leg. The picnic breaks up early so some of the parents can take Brad to the hospital. As he's being carried away he hears Ginny say, "That Brad is such a nerd. Did you see him showing off? Why doesn't he act his age? What a jerk! He wrecked the picnic."

⊞ **Positive Example**

Narrator: When he arrived at the picnic, Brad looked around for Ginny. He found her with a group standing at the edge of the softball field. Brad approached the group confidently, waited for a break in the conversation, and said "Hi" to everyone. He made a special point of smiling and saying "Hi" to Ginny. As the group was choosing teams and talking and laughing, Brad joined in, always talking on the same topic and making some comments directly to Ginny, which she responded to. During the game, Ginny hit a home run and Brad called out a compliment to her. When Brad dropped a fly ball, he laughed at the teasing he got from the other kids and clowned around a little bit.

After the game, the group headed toward the swings. As they were walking along, Brad drifted casually toward Ginny and talked with her. He offered Ginny one of the swings and they continued to talk as they were swinging. When some of the kids started throwing grass and leaves, Brad joined in, inviting Ginny to come along. They threw some leaves at each other, but when Ginny started to get a little tired of it, Brad noticed and stopped. Soon the group headed for the picnic baskets. Brad asked Ginny if she would sit by him while they ate and she did.

 **Important Points to Remember About Interacting with the Opposite Sex**

1. Carry on good conversations.

   Important points to remember about having conversations

   a. Listen about as much as you talk.

   b. Show enthusiasm and interest.

c. Make sense; stay on the topic.

d. Keep the conversation going; ask and answer questions.

2. Extend invitations.

3. Read the other person's signals.

4. Act thoughtfully.

EXERCISE 1

Narrator: Kelly sees Allie in the hall at school.

Kelly: Hi, Allie. Can I talk to you for a minute?

Allie: Hi, Kelly. I'm on my way to class, but we can talk on the way.

Kelly: Well, Ken's having a party Friday night and I was wondering if you would like to go with me.

Allie: I'd like to go, but my parents are really strict and I have to be in early.

Kelly: That's okay with me. What time do you want to be home?

Allie: (looking uncomfortable) I . . . I'm not sure . . .

Kelly: Well, how about when I pick you up I talk to your folks about what time you need to be home?

Allie: That would be great!

Kelly: OK. I'll pick you up a little after 7.

Allie: Um, 7? I don't know . . .

Kelly: Is that too early? How about 7:30? We don't want to be the first ones there.

Allie: 7:30 would be a lot better. I'll see you then. I'm looking forward to it.

Kelly: Me, too.

✔ Checklist For Exercise 1

Did Kelly . . .	Yes	No
1. Carry on a good conversation?	☐	☐
2. Extend an invitation?	☐	☐
3. Read Allie's signals?	☐	☐
4. Act thoughtfully?	☐	☐

EXERCISE 2

Narrator: Rachel is talking to her friend Lisa about a new boy in school, Greg.

Rachel: I'd sure like to get him to ask me out.

Lisa: Well, it would probably be a good idea to meet him first. He's in my math class and he's really nice. Come on, I'll introduce you right now.

Rachel: No! I have to get him to notice me. I know! Watch this. (Rachel walks by Greg, purposely bumps into him and drops her books.) Hey, look what you did!

Greg: (looking embarrassed.) Uh, sorry. I'll pick up your books. (He quickly picks up her books and leaves as fast as he can.)

Rachel: Boy, is he stuck up. He barely even looked at me. Wonder what his problem is?

✔ Checklist For Exercise 2

Did Rachel . . .	Yes	No
1. Carry on a good conversation?	☐	☐
2. Extend an invitation?	☐	☐
3. Read Greg's signals?	☐	☐
4. Act thoughtfully?	☐	☐

EXERCISE 3

Narrator: Dean and Diane have been to a movie.

Dean: You want to stop someplace and get something to eat?

Diane: Yeah, let's go to the French Chateau. Everybody says it's really classy and they have great food.

Dean: (looking embarrassed) You want to go there? That sounds kinda fancy. Nobody we know will be there.

Diane: Come on. Let's just try it.

Dean: Well, I was thinking of someplace like Dairy Queen or A&W. I don't think I have enough money for a place like the Chateau. Besides, we're not dressed up or anything.

Diane: OK. That's enough excuses. Have it your way. We'll go to some dumpy drive-in.

✔ Checklist For Exercise 3

Did Diane . . .

	Yes	No
1. Carry on a good conversation?	☐	☐
2. Extend an invitation?	☐	☐
3. Read Dean's signals?	☐	☐
4. Act thoughtfully?	☐	☐

★ Situational Role Play Evaluation Guidelines

	Situational Role Play				
	#1	**#2**	**#3**	**#4**	**#5**
1. Carry on a good conversation.	—	—	—	—	—
2. Extend an invitation.	—	—	—	—	—
3. Read the other person's signals.	—	—	—	—	—
4. Act thoughtfully.	—	—	—	—	—
Apply the Triple A Strategy	—	—	—	—	—

Lesson 11
Student Contract

Directions: Fill in the blanks with appropriate answers and check with the teacher.

In what situation will you use the skill of interacting with the opposite sex?

_____

_____

_____

With whom will you use this skill?

_____

_____

_____

What do you expect to happen when you use the skill of interacting with the opposite sex in the situation you described above?

_____

_____

_____

What might happen if you didn't use the skill of interacting with the opposite sex in this situation?

_____

_____

_____

I agree to try the skill of interacting with the opposite sex with all its important points by (date) _____ . I will do my best to perform this skill, and I will report back to my class accurately and truthfully about how I used this skill and what the outcomes were.

_____   _____
Signed by student   Signed by teacher

LESSON 12. NEGOTIATING WITH OTHERS

Review of Lesson 11 (Interacting with the Opposite Sex)

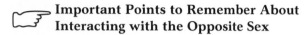 **Important Points to Remember About Interacting with the Opposite Sex**

1. Carry on good conversations.

2. Extend invitations.

3. Read the other person's signals.

4. Act thoughtfully.

Lesson 12. Negotiating with Others

⊟ Negative Example

Narrator: Rafe and Rick are trying to plan their Saturday morning.

Rafe: I want to go to the water slide. It's really fun.

Rick: I think I'd rather go to the mall. I have to look for some things for my models.

Rafe: But we can only be gone 'til noon, and if we go to the mall, you'll spend 3 hours looking at stuff and you won't buy anything.

Rick: (angrily) I buy stuff!! Besides, we can go to the water slide any time. There's a sale on at the hobby store.

Rafe: (very sharply) Big deal!! I'm calling Jack. He'll go with me.

Rick: (very angrily) Some friend you are!! Go ahead, call Jack!

Narrator: Rick leaves the room and Rafe picks up the phone to call Jack.

⊞ Positive Example

Narrator: Rafe and Rick are planning their Saturday morning.

Rafe: I want to go to the water slide. It's really fun.

Rick: I think I'd rather go to the mall. I have to look for some things for my models.

Rafe: Yeah, I heard they were having a sale at the hobby store. We have 3 hours. Why can't we could do both?

The water slide is near the mall. If I helped you look for your model parts, we'd still have time for the water slide.

Rick: Good idea! Dad could pick us up at the slide at 12:30 so we'd be home in time for lunch.

Rafe: Let's tell your dad and get going. It's almost 8:30.

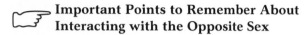 **Important Points to Remember About Negotiating with Others**

1. State your position calmly.

2. Let others state their positions.

3. Evaluate, fairly, the other person's position.

4. Compromise.

EXERCISE 1

Narrator: Joe and Juan share a locker. Juan's friends have the combination and use the locker to store their things because it is close to their classes.

Joe: Juan, I can't tell who is using our locker anymore. I'm losing things from the locker and sometimes I can't get my stuff into it because it's full of your friends' stuff. We've got to do something about this.

Juan: Don't get all upset. My friends need a place to put their stuff between classes. I use their lockers when I'm over in that part of the building, so it's only fair to let them use mine. Besides, you know these guys. It's all right.

Joe: I don't use their lockers and I lost a calculator last week. It's NOT all right with me. I don't mind if they use the locker, as long as I can get my things in too and I don't get ripped off.

Juan: I didn't know something was missing. I'll talk to them about it.

Narrator: Later.

Juan: Here's your calculator. Julio had it. He thought it was mine. He and Rob are going to clean some of their junk out of our locker. Rob says if you want to use his locker when you're over in that area, he'll give you the combination. OK?

Joe: That would be great. Thanks for talking to them.

✔ Checklist For Exercise 1

Did Juan and Joe . . . **Yes** **No**

1. State their positions calmly? ☐ ☐

2. Let the other person state his position? ☐ ☐

3. Evaluate, fairly, the other's position? ☐ ☐

4. Compromise? ☐ ☐

EXERCISE 2

Narrator: Dwight, John, and Steve are working on a landscaping job for Mr. White. They have divided the job into three parts and are working on it separately whenever they have time. To get paid, they have to complete the job in three weeks.

Dwight: You mean that John and I have worked for two weeks really hard on this project and you haven't done a thing?

Steve: Hey, I had all these other things to do. I'll get it done. Besides, what would happen if I didn't? It's not worth very much money.

John: Maybe you don't need that money, but I do. I've already done my share of the work and I want to get paid for it.

Dwight: Yeah, if we want to get paid we're going to end up doing your share. You're a jerk, Steve.

Steve: I told you, I was busy with other things. Just wait; I'll get it done.

John: Can we count on that?

Steve: (laughing as he walks away) Does a duck waddle?

Dwight: We better do his part. He's not going to get it done.

✔ Checklist For Exercise 2

Did Steve . . . **Yes** **No**

1. State his position calmly? ☐ ☐

2. Let others state their positions? ☐ ☐

3. Evaluate, fairly, the other's position? ☐ ☐

4. Compromise? ☐ ☐

EXERCISE 3

Narrator: Bob is watching a football game. His sister Allison comes into the room.

Allison: Isn't that game over yet? It's time for a program I want to see.

Bob: It's a great game. Late in the fourth quarter and tied up and my team's in great position.

Allison: I'm delighted, but I want to see something else. How much time left?

Bob: 2 minutes.

Allison: That's about 15 minutes in football time. Could I just turn it for a minute?

Bob: How about if you watch your show during time outs? But be sure to flip it back when I tell you.

Allison: OK. I can live with that for 15 minutes.

✔ Checklist For Exercise 3

Did Bob and Allison . . . **Yes** **No**

1. State their positions calmly? ☐ ☐

2. Let the other state his/her position? ☐ ☐

3. Evaluate, fairly, the other's position? ☐ ☐

4. Compromise? ☐ ☐

★ Situational Role Play Evaluation Guidelines

	Situational Role Play				
	#1	**#2**	**#3**	**#4**	**#5**
1. State your position calmly.	—	—	—	—	—
2. Let others state their positions.	—	—	—	—	—
3. Evaluate, fairly, the other's position.	—	—	—	—	—
4. Compromise.	—	—	—	—	—
Apply the Triple A Strategy	—	—	—	—	—

39

Lesson 12
Student Contract

Directions: Fill in the blanks with appropriate answers and check with the teacher.

In what situation will you use the skill of negotiating with others?

_____

_____

_____

What would you expect to happen if you didn't use this skill in the situation described above?

_____

_____

_____

With whom will you use the skill of negotiating with others?

_____

_____

_____

What do you expect to happen when you use this skill?

_____

_____

_____

I agree to try to use the skill of negotiating with others with all its important points by (date) _____ . I will do my best to negotiate with others, and I will report back to my class accurately and truthfully about how I used this skill and what the outcomes were.

_____   _____
Signed by student   Signed by teacher

LESSON 13. BEING LEFT OUT

Review of Lesson 12 (Negotiating with Others)

☞ **Important Points to Remember About Negotiating with Others**

1. State your position calmly.

2. Let others state their positions.

3. Evaluate, fairly, the other person's position.

4. Compromise.

Lesson 14. Being Left Out

⊟ **Negative Example**

Narrator: Roger slams the receiver of the phone down in disgust. His sister, Darla, is watching.

Roger: I didn't want to go to their stinking party anyway. They're a bunch of jerks. Boy, see if I ever do anything for them again.

Darla: Who was on the phone?

Roger: Ken. Stupid Kenneth.

Darla: What did he say that upset you so much?

Roger: He told me about the party he and Dan had last night.

Darla: And you weren't invited?

Roger: (pushing Darla aside and rushing toward his room) Right, but I don't need them!! They're stupid!!

⊞ **Positive Example**

Roger: (talking on the phone) Yeah! I'll bet you really had fun last night, Ken. I sure would have liked you to call me. Next time you and Dan want to get together like that, maybe we could use my house. We have a big basement and I have good sound equipment. (pause while listening) What are you going to be doing later this afternoon? (pause while listening) Well, I was going to the mall and thought maybe you wanted to go along. (pause while listening) Well, maybe we could do it next week. (pause while listening) OK, I'll talk to you later. (hangs up)

Darla: Sounds like Ken and Dan had a good time last night.

Roger: Yeah, they did.

Darla: Why weren't you invited?

Roger: It just happened in the group they were with and I just wasn't there at the time.

Darla: Are you really going to the mall later today?

Roger: Yeah. But Ken can't go. He has to work at home.

Darla: Can I go with you?

Roger: Sure.

☞ **Important Points to Remember About Being Left Out**

1. Try to decide why you were left out.

2. Try to resolve the problem:
   a. Apologize and change your behavior.
   b. Ask to be included.

3. If you are still left out, find other friends or something else to do.

EXERCISE 1

Narrator: Lisa sees a group of her friends talking quietly and seriously in the hall at school. They stop talking when she joins them.

Lisa: Hi. What's going on?

Lynn: Nothing.

Lisa: Did I interrupt something?

Jean: (looking guilty) No, nothing, really.

Lisa: It seems that way. Did I do something to make you guys mad?

Kay: Well, now that you mention it, Jean says you hung up on her when she called you last night.

Lisa: Oh, Jean, I'm sorry! I forgot to call you back! My mom made me get off the phone real fast because she needed to make a call, and I just forgot to get back to you.

Lynn: You know, I thought it was something like that.

Narrator: They all walk off together.

✔ Checklist For Exercise 1

Did Lisa . . .   **Yes   No**

1. Try to decide why she was left out?   ☐   ☐

2. Try to resolve the problem: ☐   ☐
   a. Apologize and change her
      behavior?
   b. Ask to be included?

3. Still feel left out and find other   ☐   ☐
   friends or something else to do?

EXERCISE 2

Narrator: Mike starts to sit down next to Ted in the lunchroom.

Ted: Whoa! all the seats at this end of the table are taken. Sorry, man.

Mike: That's what you said yesterday when I tried to sit here.

Ted: Don't take it wrong. We've all just been friends for a long time and we like to sit together at lunch.

Narrator: Mike goes to the next table where Mac and Rich are sitting.

Mike: Mind if I sit here?

Mac: Go ahead. We were just talking about the game tonight. Are you going?

Mike: I hope so. I don't have a ride yet.

Rich: Want to ride with us?

Mike: Sure! Thanks!

✔ Checklist For Exercise 2

Did Mike . . .   **Yes   No**

1. Try to decide why he was left out?   ☐   ☐

2. Try to resolve the problem: ☐   ☐
   a. Apologize and change his
      behavior?

   b. Ask to be included?   ☐   ☐

3. Still feel left out and find other
   friends or something else to do?

EXERCISE 3

Narrator: Tammy wants to belong to a club at school, but it's a special club and you have to be invited to join. She finds out that only two people voted to invite her, so she can't become a member. Tammy thinks to herself: I'm so embarrassed! Hardly anybody voted for me. They must all hate me. They're probably all laughing about it now. Who cares! They're just a bunch of stuck up rich kids and I'm never going to speak to any of them again!

✔ Checklist For Exercise 3

Did Tammy . . .   **Yes   No**

1. Try to decide why she was left out?   ☐   ☐

2. Try to resolve the problem: ☐   ☐
   a. Apologize and/or change her
      behavior?
   b. Ask to be included?

3. Still feel left out and find other   ☐   ☐
   friends or something else to do?

★ Situational Role Play Evaluation Guidelines

	Situational Role Play				
	#1	**#2**	**#3**	**#4**	**#5**
1. Try to decide why you were left out.	—	—	—	—	—
2. Try to resolve the problem: a. Apologize and/or change your behavior. b. Ask to be included.	—	—	—	—	—
3. If you are still left out, find other friends or something else to do.					
Apply the Triple A Strategy	—	—	—	—	—

42

Lesson 13
Student Contract

Directions: Since no one knows when a situation will come up where you will feel left out, we can't write a contract to use this skill by a certain date. Instead, here is a report form to use the next time you feel you have been left out. Fill it out and report back to your teacher and class about the outcomes.

In what situation did you use the skill of handling rejection?

_____

_____

_____

_____

What might have happened if you hadn't used this skill in that situation?

_____

_____

_____

_____

What happened when you used the skill of handling rejection?

_____

_____

_____

_____

I agree to try the skill of handling rejection the next time I feel left out. I will report back to my class accurately and truthfully about how I used this skill and what the outcomes were.

_____   _____
Signed by student   Signed by teacher

LESSON 14. HANDLING PRESSURE FROM PEERS

Review of Lesson 13 (Being Left Out)

☞ Important Points to Remember About Being Left Out

1. Try to decide why you were left out.

2. Try to resolve the problem:
   a. Apologize and change your behavior.
   b. Ask to be included.

3. If you are still left out, find other friends or something else to do.

Lesson 14. Handling Pressure from Peers

⊟ Negative Example

Narrator: Alan is collecting his books at his locker after school. A group of his friends gathers around him.

Steve: Hey, man, we just heard the good news. Party at your house tonight!

Alan: What party?

Steve: We heard your parents are out of town for the weekend, so we'll be over about eight to help you celebrate!

Pete: Yeah, it's your duty to have a party if you've got that whole house to yourself and no parents to get in the way.

Alan: Well, I don't know. . . . This is the first time they've left me in charge. What if something happens, like we break something or the neighbors complain?

Tom: What a wimp! That's part of the fun. You never know what might happen. You're not scared are you?

Alan: Who me? No! Of course not!

Steve: Good, then it's all set. We'll be over about eight. Make sure there's plenty in the fridge.

Narrator: Alan's friends leave. Alan is worried!

Alan: (to himself) What have I gotten myself into? My parents are going to kill me if they find out. They'll never trust me again. Besides, I wanted to go to the game tonight, not stay home. What am I going to do?

⊞ Positive Example

Narrator: Alan is at his locker after school when his friends approach.

Steve: We heard the news about your parents being away this weekend. We'll be over about eight to help you celebrate!

Tom: Yeah, we know you won't let your old buddies down when you have a chance like this to entertain.

Alan: Sorry, I've got other plans tonight. I'm going to the game. Want to meet me there?

Tom: What's the matter? Afraid you'll get in trouble if you have a party while your folks are gone? Are you chicken or what?

Alan: Nah, I promised I'd be responsible and I like being in charge so that's what I plan to do. Why don't you give me a call if you decide to go to the game?

Narrator: Alan closes the door to his locker and walks away, leaving the group talking among themselves.

☞ Important Points to Remember About Handling Pressure from Peers

1. Ask yourself, "Is this something I should do or really want to do?"

2. If it is something you shouldn't or don't want to do, choose a way to say no:
   a. Give a reason.
   b. Suggest something else to do.
   c. Change the subject.
   d. Stall.
   e. Give permission to someone else.

3. If you are still feeling pressured, say "no" and leave the situation.

EXERCISE 1

Narrator: Val and Liz are in a department store.

Liz: I really love these new sweaters. I wish I could afford one.

Val: You can. Just use your five-finger discount.

Liz: You mean steal it? No way!

Val: It's not really stealing. They expect to lose a certain amount of stuff that way. That's why the price is so high. Besides, you won't get caught.

Liz: I'm not going to do it. It *is* stealing, and if I do get caught my parents would kill me and I'd die of embarrassment and probably have to pay a fine or something. Besides, it's just not right. Let's go home. I'm tired of shopping.

✔ Checklist For Exercise 1

Did Liz . . .   Yes   No

1. Ask herself, "Is this something I should ☐ ☐
   do or really want to do?"

2. Choose a way to say no?   ☐ ☐
   a. Give a reason.
   b. Suggest something else to do.
   c. Change the subject.
   d. Stall.
   e. Give permission to someone else.

3. Say "no" and leave the situation?   ☐ ☐

EXERCISE 2

Narrator: It's freshman initiation week at Doug's school. He and some other sophomores are planning practical jokes to play on new students.

Stu: I've got a good one! Let's take that little guy Marty blindfolded into the swimming pool area, make him climb up on the high dive and jump.

Andy: Great! Only let's tie his hands, too, and have the lights out.

Doug: I don't know, that sounds kinda dangerous.

Stu: So what? That's what makes it exciting.

Doug: Well . . .

Andy: Of course if you're afraid of getting in trouble . . .

Doug: No, of course not. I guess it's OK.

✔ Checklist For Exercise 2

Did Doug . . .   Yes   No

1. Ask himself, "Is this something I should ☐ ☐
   do or really want to do?"

2. Choose a way to say no?   ☐ ☐
   a. Give a reason.
   b. Suggest something else to do.
   c. Change the subject.
   d. Stall.
   e. Give permission to someone else.

3. Say "no" and leave the situation?   ☐ ☐

EXERCISE 3

Narrator: Leon is riding around in a car with a bunch of other guys on a Saturday night. Somebody starts passing a joint around. It comes to Leon.

Leon: I'll pass, you go ahead.

Ty: Come on, chump, take a hit.

Leon: Later. (takes the joint and passes it on; as he does this he says to Richie, the driver) How long did you say you'd had this car?

Richie: About 2 weeks.

Leon: Man, it's a great car. How much did you pay for it?

(The group continues to discuss Richie's car.)

✔ Checklist For Exercise 3

Did Leon . . .   Yes   No

1. Ask himself, "Is this something I should ☐ ☐
   do or really want to do?"

2. Choose a way to say no?   ☐ ☐
   a. Give a reason.
   b. Suggest something else to do.
   c. Change the subject.
   d. Stall.
   e. Give permission to someone else.

3. Say "no" and leave the situation?   ☐ ☐

★ Situational Role Play Evaluation Guidelines

	Situational Role Play				
	#1	#2	#3	#4	#5
1. Ask yourself, "Is this something I should do or really want to do?"	—	—	—	—	—

2. If it is something you shouldn't or do not want to do, choose a way to say no: — — — — —

    a. Give a reason.
    b. Suggest something else to do.
    c. Change the subject.

d. Stall.
e. Give permission to someone else.

3. If you are still feeling pressured, say "no" and leave the situation.   — — — — —

Apply the Triple A Strategy   — — — — —

Lesson 14
Student Contract

Directions: Since no one knows when you will have to handle group pressure, we can't write a contract to use this skill by a certain date. Instead, here is a report form to use the next time you have to handle group pressure. Fill it out and report back to your teacher about the outcomes.

In what situation did you use the skill of handling group pressure?

_____

_____

_____

How did you use the skill of handling group pressure?

_____

_____

_____

What might have happened if you hadn't used this skill in this situation?

_____

_____

_____

What happened when you used the skill of handling group pressure?

_____

_____

_____

I agree to try the skill of handling group pressure the next time I feel pressured to do something I shouldn't or don't want to do. I will report back to my class accurately and truthfully about how I used this skill and what the outcomes were.

_____   _____
Signed by student   Signed by teacher

LESSON 15. EXPRESSING ANGER

Review of Lesson 14 (Handling Group Pressure)

☞ **Important Points to Remember About Handling Group Pressure**

1. Ask yourself, "Is this something I should do or really want to do?"

2. If it is something you shouldn't or don't want to do, choose a way to say no:
   a. Give a reason.
   b. Suggest something else to do.
   c. Change the subject.
   d. Stall.
   e. Give permission to someone else.

3. If you are still feeling pressured, say "no" and leave the situation.

Lesson 16. Expressing Anger

⊟ **Negative Example**

Narrator: J.C. is standing in the lunch line holding his tray when Tommy turns quickly and accidentally knocks the tray out of J.C.'s hand, spilling the soup on the floor.

J.C.: (pushing Tommy out of the line) You clumsy oaf!

Tommy: What did you do that for?

J.C.: You made me spill my soup! You klutz!

Tommy: I couldn't help it! It was an accident!

J.C.: You're an idiot! (pushing Tommy again) I'm going to get you after school!

Narrator: Tommy moves away and gets in line again. He starts complaining to the kids around him about how J.C. treated him.

⊞ **Positive Example**

Narrator: J.C. is standing in the lunch line when Tommy turns quickly and accidentally knocks the tray out of J.C.'s hand.

J.C.: Whoa, big guy! Look out there!

Tommy: Oh! Sorry, it was an accident.

J.C.: (looking angry) I know, but what a mess!

Tommy: I'm really sorry, J.C. I'll help you clean it up.

J.C.: Thanks. Would you hand me a clean tray, too, please?

Tommy: Sure. Boy, do I feel clumsy.

J.C.: Don't worry about it. (in kidding tone) Just remind me to give you plenty of room next time we're in line together.

☞ **Important Points to Remember About Expressing Anger**

1. Stay in control of your behavior.

2. Be firm but fair in stating your position.

3. Be respectful and polite.

4. Try not to injure people or hurt their feelings.

EXERCISE 1

Narrator: The team is practicing for a big game. Because it is important that they get their plays down right, the practice is becoming very tense. Ron misses a play and George yells at him.

George: Ron, you idiot! Can't you get this play down right?

Ron: Come on, George. This is practice, remember? This is where we make mistakes and correct them. Where do you get off calling me an idiot?

George: You are an idiot, and if you can't do it right you don't belong on the team.

Ron: (shaking his head and walking away) I can't believe you! Does the coach know you're doing his job for him?

George: If you could play as well as you talk I wouldn't have to.

✔ **Checklist For Exercise 1**

Did George . . .   **Yes   No**

1. Stay in control of his behavior?   ☐   ☐

48

2. State his position firmly but fairly? ☐ ☐

3. Treat Ron respectfully and politely? ☐ ☐

4. Try not to injure Ron or hurt his feelings? ☐ ☐

EXERCISE 2

Narrator: Lydia heard from a friend that Vera had started a rumor about her. Lydia is very angry.

Lydia: Vera, you started a rumor about me and I don't like it a bit. People like you ought to be put away somewhere. You're nothing but a liar. (Lydia comes at Vera in a threatening way.)

Vera: Hey, stay away from me! I don't know what you're talking about!

Lydia: Tell everybody you take back what you said or I'm going to tear your hair out!

Vera: You're crazy! (turns to run)

Lydia: Come back, you . . . you . . .

✔ **Checklist For Exercise 2**

Did Lydia . . .   **Yes   No**

1. Stay in control of her behavior? ☐ ☐

2. State her position firmly but fairly? ☐ ☐

3. Treat Vera respectfully and politely? ☐ ☐

4. Try not to injure Vera or hurt her feelings? ☐ ☐

EXERCISE 3

Narrator: Jonathan borrowed one of Brandon's computer discs. Somehow Jonathan erased all the games on the disc. Brandon is very upset.

Brandon: Jonathan, when I loaned you that disc I expected you to take care of it, but now all the games are gone.

Jonathan: I know, and I'm really sorry. I feel terrible about it. I was using a computer at school and somehow I just erased everything.

Brandon: I know you feel bad about it, Jonathan. Got any ideas for getting me another set of games?

Jonathan: Well, I know some guys that have some of the games. I think they'd let us copy them. I could put a note on the board in my computer class and see if we can come up with the rest.

Brandon: That's a good start. I can get some from friends, too. Do you have time to copy some during your class?

Jonathan: I'll do it during free time until we fill the disc up. I'm glad you aren't still mad at me, Brandon.

Brandon: I've done some dumb things on the computer myself.

✔ **Checklist For Exercise 3**

Did Brandon . . .   **Yes   No**

1. Stay in control of his behavior? ☐ ☐

2. State his position firmly but fairly? ☐ ☐

3. Treat Jonathan respectfully and politely? ☐ ☐

4. Try not to injure Jonathan or hurt his feelings? ☐ ☐

★ **Situational Role Play Evaluation Guidelines**

	Situational Role Play				
	#1	#2	#3	#4	#5
1. Stay in control of your behavior.	—	—	—	—	—
2. State your position firmly but fairly.	—	—	—	—	—
3. Be respectful and polite.	—	—	—	—	—
4. Try not to injure people or hurt their feelings.	—	—	—	—	—
Apply the Triple A Strategy	—	—	—	—	—

Lesson 15
Student Contract

Directions: Since no one knows when you will be in a situation where you will express anger, we can't write a contract to use this skill by a certain date. Instead, here is a report form to use the next time you have to express anger. Fill it out and report back to your teacher about the outcomes.

In what situation did you use the skill of expressing anger?

_____

_____

_____

How did you use this skill?

_____

_____

_____

What might have happened if you hadn't used this skill in this situation?

_____

_____

_____

What happened when you used the skill of expressing anger?

_____

_____

_____

I agree to use the skill of expressing anger with all its important points the next time a situation calls for use of this skill. I will report back to my class accurately and truthfully about how I used this skill and what the outcomes were.

_____   _____
Signed by student   Signed by teacher

LESSON 16. COPING WITH AGGRESSION

Review of Lesson 15 (Expressing Anger)

☞ **Important Points to Remember About Expressing Anger**

1. Stay in control of your behavior.

2. Be firm but fair in stating your position.

3. Be respectful and polite.

4. Try not to injure people or hurt their feelings.

Lesson 16. Coping with Aggression

⊟ **Negative Example**

Narrator: Gary has just been through the lunch line and places his tray on a table where no one is sitting. As he sits down, Paul comes up to him.

Paul: (angrily) What are you doing here? This is our table!

Gary: I didn't see your name on it.

Paul: This is always our table, we always sit here. (looks threatening) Get out of here!

Gary: I have as much right to be here as you do!

Paul: (pushing Gary on the shoulder) Get out of here before you get hurt!

Gary: I'm not leaving.

Paul: (pushing Gary harder) Get moving before I beat you up!

Gary: You and whose army!

Narrator: By this time, Paul is really angry and hits Gary on the shoulder, pushes him off the bench and onto the floor. Gary gets up ready to fight. They fight for a short time until Mr. Birch comes over.

Mr. Birch: All right, you guys, break it up!

Paul: He started it!

Gary: I did not! All I did was sit down at this table. He shoved me.

Paul: (threatening Gary with a gesture) You started it!

Mr. Birch: All right, both of you, come with me to the office. Paul, you're always in trouble.

Gary: But I didn't do anything.

Mr. Birch: You were in a fight, weren't you?

⊞ **Positive Example**

Narrator: Gary finds a seat in the lunch room. As he sits down Paul approaches.

Paul: Get out of here! This is our table!

Gary: Well, I'm sorry. I didn't know you had reserved a table in the lunch room.

Paul: (looking threatening) Well, we have. This is always our table. You better leave.

Gary: All right. No big deal. There's plenty of room over there.

Paul: (pushing Gary on the shoulder) Hurry up!

Narrator: Ignoring Paul, Gary picks up his tray and leaves. When he gets to the next table, the boy he sits next to pats him on the back.

Boy: Welcome back to civilization. Didn't anyone tell you about the "Table of the Apes"?

Gary: No. It just looked like an empty table to me.

Boy: Well, now you know their rule: "No humans allowed."

Narrator: Gary joins in the laughter with everyone at the table.

☞ **Important Points to Remember About Coping with Aggression**

1. Decide whether someone may get out of control.

2. Think about the consequences.

3. Leave the situation or drop the discussion.

4. Get help when needed.

EXERCISE 1

Narrator: Rick has been talking to Susan near her locker. They are both laughing and having a good time. When the conversation ends, Rick walks down the hall. Randy walks up behind him.

Randy: (pushing Rick from behind) What are you doing talking to my girlfriend?

Rick: What do you mean?

Randy: Susan's my girl.

Rick: I didn't know that. Does that mean she can't talk to anyone?

Randy: It means you ought to leave her alone, because if you don't, I'm going to break your face.

Rick: Hey, Randy, don't get all upset. I wasn't asking her out or anything. All we were doing was talking about biology class.

Randy: (poking Rick in the chest) I'm putting you on notice right now, stay away.

Rick: (to himself: Reasoning with this guy is hopeless.) It's time for class, I got the message.

Narrator: Randy and Rick leave.

✔ Checklist For Exercise 1

Did Rick . . .   Yes   No

1. Decide whether someone might lose control?   ☐ ☐

2. Think about the consequences?   ☐ ☐

3. Leave the situation or drop the discussion?   ☐ ☐

4. Get help when needed?   ☐ ☐

EXERCISE 2

Narrator: A gang of boys makes Julio and some of his friends pay them 50 cents every day. They say that if Julio and others don't pay they will beat them up or slash their bike tires or break the windows of their houses or do some other damage. Julio is tired of the situation. He never gets to eat lunch because he never has enough money. He decides next time the gang tries to get his money he will fight them.

✔ Checklist For Exercise 2

Did Julio . . .   Yes   No

1. Decide whether someone may lose control?   ☐ ☐

2. Think about the consequences?   ☐ ☐

3. Leave the situation or drop the discussion?   ☐ ☐

4. Get help when needed?   ☐ ☐

EXERCISE 3

Narrator: Sam and Matt are good friends, even though Matt has a pretty quick temper. They are walking home from the bus stop.

Sam: I couldn't believe that weird outfit your sister wore to school today, man. I mean, green hair? She's ugly enough without . . .

Matt: (grabbing Sam by the front of his shirt and shoving him against a storefront) Who do you think you are, talking about my sister like that?

Sam: Hey, Matt, it's me! Your buddy, Sam. Let me go. I'm sorry. Forget it.

(Matt lets go of Sam but still looks angry.)

Sam: I'm really sorry, Matt. Let's just drop it, OK?

Matt: OK.

Sam: So what are you doing this weekend?

✔ Checklist For Exercise 3

Did Sam . . .   Yes   No

1. Decide whether someone may lose control?   ☐ ☐

2. Think about the consequences?   ☐ ☐

3. Leave the situation or drop the discussion?   ☐ ☐

4. Get help when needed?   ☐ ☐

★ Situational Role Play Evaluation Guidelines

	Situational Role Play				
	#1	#2	#3	#4	#5
1. Decide whether someone may lose control.	___	___	___	___	___

2. Think about the
   consequences.   — — — — —

3. Leave the situation or drop
   the discussion.   — — — — —

4. Get help when needed.   — — — — —

Apply the Triple A Strategy   — — — — —

Lesson 16
Student Contract

Directions: Since no one knows when you will have to cope with aggression, we can't write a contract to use this skill by a certain date. Instead, here is a report form to use the next time you have to cope with agression. Fill it out and report back to your teacher about the outcomes.

In what situation did you use the skill of coping with aggression?

_____

_____

_____

How did you cope with aggression?

_____

_____

_____

What happened when you used the skill of coping with aggression?

_____

_____

_____

What might have happened if you hadn't used this skill in this situation?

_____

_____

_____

I agree to use the skill of coping with aggression should a situation arise where someone becomes aggressive with me. I will report back to my class accurately and truthfully about how I used this skill and what the outcomes were.

_____   _____
Signed by student   Signed by teacher

LESSON 17. GETTING AN ADULT'S ATTENTION

Review of Lesson 16 (Coping with Aggression)

☞ **Important Points to Remember About Coping with Aggression**

1. Decide whether someone may get out of control.

2. Think about the consequences.

3. Leave the situation or drop the discussion.

4. Get help when needed.

Lesson 17. Getting an Adult's Attention

⊟ **Negative Example**

Narrator: Andy is enrolled in a class which will allow him to enter an electrician's apprentice program when he gets out of high school. The instructor for the class is Ms. Shirley Weeks. Andy is supposed to be working on an assignment, but he is completely lost. He drums his fingers on his desk. He turns around to ask another student what he is supposed to be doing. Ms. Weeks seems to be annoyed by Andy's activity in class.

Ms. Weeks: (curtly) Andy! Turn around and get to work!

Narrator: Andy is embarrassed, so he won't tell her he doesn't know what to do. He pages through his book for a while. Then he raises his hand, but Ms. Weeks is working at her desk and doesn't see him. Finally in desperation he acts again.

Andy: (sarcastically) Hey, Shirley! What am I supposed to be doing here?

Narrator: Some of the students in the class laugh, but others seem annoyed at the interruption. Ms. Weeks comes over to Andy's table.

Ms. Weeks: Now that you have disrupted the class, what's the problem?

Andy: I don't get what we're supposed to do.

Ms. Weeks: Fine. I'll tell you. But next time listen when I give the assignment. (said firmly) And my name is Ms. Weeks, please.

⊞ **Positive Example**

Narrator: Andy is having trouble getting started on the exercise assigned by Ms. Weeks. He raises his hand while still turning the pages in the book to find the assignment. Ms. Weeks is busy at her desk preparing the next assignment and does not see Andy's raised hand. Andy waits quietly for a few minutes and decides he'll have to go to Ms. Weeks's desk to get her attention.

Andy: (approaching the desk) Excuse me, Ms. Weeks, I didn't understand the assignment you gave. What page was the exercise on?

Ms. Weeks: You are supposed to read the rules on pages 46 to 50 and then apply the rules to the problems on page 150.

Andy: Thank you. (returns to his table and begins work)

☞ **Important Points to Remember About Getting an Adult's Attention**

1. Choose a good time to ask for help.

2. Call the adult by the name he or she prefers.

3. Use a respectful tone of voice.

4. Demonstrate politeness and good manners.

EXERCISE 1

Narrator: Sara is having a hard time filling the napkin dispensers correctly at the fast food restaurant where she works. She would like her supervisor to show her how to do it, but she's embarrassed to ask for help. After a while, she slams a dispenser on the counter and shouts, "This is stupid!"

✔ **Checklist For Exercise 1**

Did Sara . . .	Yes	No
1. Choose a good time to ask for help?	☐	☐
2. Call her supervisor by her preferred name?	☐	☐
3. Use a respectful tone of voice?	☐	☐

4. Demonstrate politeness and good manners? ☐ ☐

EXERCISE 2

Narrator: As the teacher is lecturing, Jenny needs to have point explained. She raises her hand but the teacher doesn't see her. She keeps her hand up patiently, and the teacher eventually says, "Jot down your question on a piece of paper for now. We will go over questions after I've finished lecturing." When the lecture is completed, Jenny waits for the teacher to call for questions and has hers prepared.

✔ Checklist For Exercise 2

Did Jenny . . .   **Yes   No**

1. Choose a good time to ask for help? ☐ ☐

2. Call her teacher by his preferred name? ☐ ☐

3. Use a respectful tone of voice? ☐ ☐

4. Demonstrate politeness and good manners? ☐ ☐

EXERCISE 3

Narrator: Sam comes racing in the door after soccer practice, talking a mile a minute in a loud voice. His dad is talking to a neighbor.

Sam: Dad, Dad! Guess what? I get to start in the game on Saturday! Do you think you can come to the game? It would be great if you could because I . . .

Dad: (looking annoyed) Excuse me, Paul. Sam, I'm talking to Paul about a petition he wants me to sign and you're making it impossible for us to carry on this conversation.

Sam: (sarcastically) Well, excuse me!

✔ Checklist For Exercise 3

Did Sam . . .   **Yes   No**

1. Choose a good time to talk to his dad? ☐ ☐

2. Call his dad by his preferred title or name? ☐ ☐

3. Use a respectful tone of voice? ☐ ☐

4. Demonstrate politeness and good manners? ☐ ☐

★ Situational Role Play Evaluation Guidelines

	Situational Role Play				
	#1	**#2**	**#3**	**#4**	**#5**
1. Choose a good time to ask for help.	—	—	—	—	—
2. Call the adult by the name he or she prefers.	—	—	—	—	—
3. Use a respectful tone of voice.	—	—	—	—	—
4. Demonstrate politeness and good manners.	—	—	—	—	—
Apply the Triple A Strategy	—	—	—	—	—

Lesson 17
Student Contract

Directions: Fill in the blanks with appropriate responses and check with the teacher.

In what situation will you use the skill of getting an adult's attention?

_____

_____

What might happen if you didn't use this skill in that situation?

_____

_____

With whom will you use this skill?

_____

_____

This adult prefers to be called _____ .

What method does this adult prefer you to use to get attention?

_____

_____

What do you expect to happen when you use this skill?

_____

_____

I agree to try this skill with all its important points by (date) _____ . I will do my best to get an adult's attention in the acceptable way, and I will report back to my class accurately and truthfully about how I used this skill and what the outcomes were.

_____   _____
Signed by student   Signed by teacher

LESSON 18. DISAGREEING WITH ADULTS

Review of Lesson 17 (Getting an Adult's Attention)

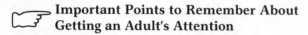 **Important Points to Remember About Getting an Adult's Attention**

1. Choose a good time to ask for help.

2. Call the adult by the name he or she prefers.

3. Use a respectful tone of voice.

4. Demonstrate politeness and good manners.

Lesson 18. Disagreeing with Adults

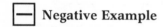 **Negative Example**

Narrator: Chris has a part-time job at The Department Store as a sales clerk after school and on Saturdays. The job requires that each clerk participate in training seminars to improve sales. The seminars are held every other Saturday morning at 8:30 a.m. This Saturday morning Chris strolls into work with her co-worker Darla.

Darla: Oh, no! I just remembered, we get our reports on sales ideas back today.

Chris: No sweat. I'm sure I aced it. I even took notes on what we were supposed to do and recopied it and everything.

Darla: Oh, yeah? What got into you?

Chris: (shrugs) I don't know. Just brilliant, I guess.

Mr. Flowers: Good morning. As promised, I have your reports to hand back. (starts handing back papers) You will notice that I have made some comments about our sales policy as they relate to your ideas.

Chris: Darla! What did you get?

Darla: (amazed) He says I did very well and they are going to use one of my ideas! I don't do this well on papers in school!

Chris: That's what you get for hanging out with me.

Narrator: Chris gets her paper last. She is shocked at what she sees.

Darla: What did he say about your ideas?

Chris: He says I didn't do the job right! And if he were a teacher he would have given me an "unsatisfactory." (waving her hand and calling) Mr. Flowers! Mr. Flowers! What's going on here? What's wrong with my paper?

Mr. Flowers: Chris, I was just explaining to the group, when you interrupted, that we don't have time to discuss individual questions today. I'll explain my comments to you individually after your work shift this afternoon.

Chris: (interrupting again) Well, that won't do! I did everything you said to do and you made these lousy comments. I want to know what *your* problem is!

Mr. Flowers: Chris, we aren't going to take time to talk about this now. I'll talk to you after work this afternoon!

Chris: It's not fair! I did exactly what you said and you found some way to mess me up!

Mr. Flowers: I'm afraid that if you can't calm down, you won't be able to meet our customers today. (forcefully) For the *last time*, I'll talk to you after work.

Chris: (getting up and starting to leave) Not today, you won't! My pleasure, I need a day off! (walks out of the room)

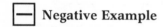 **Positive Example**

Narrator: Chris has received her paper from Mr. Flowers. She is very upset.

Chris: (to herself) I can't believe this! (raises her hand) Mr. Flowers?

Mr. Flowers: Yes, Chris.

Chris: I don't understand these comments. I worked harder on this report than I ever worked on a report in school and I know I followed the directions you gave us.

Mr Flowers: We won't be able to go over individual questions today. You can see me after your work shift this afternoon. I'll talk it over with you then.

Chris: Thank you. I'll see you at 4:30, then.

Narrator: On the way to their work stations after the sales meeting, Chris and Darla exchange comments.

Darla: What are you going to say? Are you going to tell him off?

Chris: No, I've been thinking about it and I'm going to show him my notes on the assignment and prove I did just what he said to do.

Darla: Good luck!

Narrator: At 4:30, Chris looks for Mr. Flowers in the office area of the store.

Chris: (calmly and respectfully) Mr. Flowers, here are the notes I used for the report. I think I did exactly what you told us to do. So I don't see why you made the comments you did.

Mr Flowers: You did take good notes, Chris, and you did follow directions. But what did you use for reference materials?

Chris: The company policy manual. Why?

Mr. Flowers: Your report is almost an exact copy of the company policy manual, isn't it?

Chris: I changed some things. Is that a problem?

Mr. Flowers: In this case, it's a serious problem. The purpose of the report was to involve employees in creating new sales ideas that fit within company policy. Not to test them on their knowledge of company policy. You didn't tell me your ideas. You told me what company policy is.

Chris: So you're saying I did poorly because I didn't use my own ideas?

Mr. Flowers: That's right, Chris. We want our trainees to think about their positions so they can improve their jobs and help the company grow.

Chris: In school, I always just copied things from books in my reports. Could I rewrite the report? I have some good ideas for displaying the merchandise in my section. I really think I understand what to do now.

Mr Flowers: If you can have the report back by Monday, I'll be glad to take a second look at it. It may change how we do things in your section.

Chris: Thanks. I'll get it done by Monday.

Important Points to Remember About Disagreeing with Adults

1. Choose or ask for a good time to talk.

2. Be prepared to tell your side of the problem.

3. Use a calm, respectful tone of voice.

4. Listen to the adult's position.

5. Come to an agreement.

EXERCISE 1

Narrator: John is in history class.

Mr. Reed: My grade book shows that you are missing the assignment on the War of 1812.

John: I'm sure that's wrong! I turned that in a couple of weeks ago. I remember because it's the only assignment I've turned in so far this term.

Mr. Reed: I haven't been able to locate it. If you would come in after school . . .

John: (interrupting) Forget it. Just give me an F and get it over with.

✔ Checklist For Exercise 1

Did John . . .   Yes   No

1. Choose or ask for a good time to talk?   ☐   ☐

2. Prepare to tell his side of the problem?   ☐   ☐

3. Use a calm, respectful tone of voice?   ☐   ☐

4. Listen to the adult's position?   ☐   ☐

5. Come to an agreement?   ☐   ☐

EXERCISE 2

Narrator: Ms. Gibson has informed Kevin that he will have to work on Saturday. Kevin stays after work to talk about it.

Kevin: Ms. Gibson, I think there's been a mistake. I checked with you last week and you said I could have Saturday off.

Ms. Gibson: Let's see. I don't remember talking to you about it, and it's not marked on the schedule that way.

Kevin: I know Saturday is the busiest day, and I wouldn't mind working Saturday, but I have to go to my sister's graduation.

Ms. Gibson: Oh, now I remember! You did clear that with me. I'll get someone else to work Saturday. Next time, please remind me to make the schedule change as soon as it is agreed upon.

Kevin: (relieved) Sure, thanks. I had hoped we could straighten this out.

✔ Checklist For Exercise 2

Did Kevin . . .   **Yes   No**

1. Choose or ask for a good time to talk?   ☐ ☐

2. Prepare to tell his side of the problem?   ☐ ☐

3. Use a calm, respectful tone of voice?   ☐ ☐

4. Listen to the adult's position?   ☐ ☐

5. Come to an agreement?   ☐ ☐

EXERCISE 3

Narrator: Jackie's cousin, Paul, is visiting her from out of town. He has permission from the office to visit her at school. But when they walk into Mr. Spencer's class, he asks Paul to leave.

Jackie: Excuse me, Mr. Spencer, I don't understand why he can't stay.

Mr. Spencer: We're having a test today, as you know, and I have found that guests are distracting. Now it's time to get started. The test takes all period.

Jackie: I really think this is unfair. When can I talk to you about it?

Mr. Spencer: Not now. How about after school?

Jackie: OK. If we didn't have a test today I'd walk right out of here, but I guess I'd better stay.

Mr. Spencer: I'd say that's a good choice. Now, we need to get started.

✔ Checklist For Exercise 3

Did Jackie . . .   **Yes   No**

1. Choose or ask for a good time to talk?   ☐ ☐

2. Prepare to tell her side of the problem?   ☐ ☐

3. Use a calm, respectful tone of voice?   ☐ ☐

4. Listen to the adult's position?   ☐ ☐

5. Come to an agreement?   ☐ ☐

★ Situational Role Play Evaluation Guidelines

	Situational Role Play				
	#1	#2	#3	#4	#5
1. Choose or ask for a good time to talk.	—	—	—	—	—
2. Be prepared to tell your side of the problem.	—	—	—	—	—
3. Use a calm, respectful tone.	—	—	—	—	—
4. Listen to the adult's position.	—	—	—	—	—
5. Come to an agreement.	—	—	—	—	—
Apply the Triple A Strategy	—	—	—	—	—

Lesson 18
Student Contract

Directions: Fill in the blanks with appropriate answers and check with your teacher.

In what situation will you use the skill of disagreeing with adults?

_____

_____

_____

What do you think might happen if you don't use this skill in that situation?

_____

_____

_____

With whom will you use this skill?

_____

_____

_____

What do you expect to happen when you use this skill?

_____

_____

_____

I agree to try this skill with all its important points by (date) _____ . I will do my best to disagree with adults in an acceptable way, and I will report back to my class accurately and truthfully about how I used this skill and what the outcomes were.

_____   _____
Signed by student   Signed by teacher

LESSON 19. RESPONDING TO REQUESTS FROM PARENTS, TEACHERS, AND EMPLOYERS

Review of Lesson 18 (Disagreeing with Adults)

 **Important Points to Remember About Disagreeing with Adults**

1. Choose or ask for a good time to talk.

2. Be prepared to tell your side of the problem.

3. Use a calm, respectful tone of voice.

4. Listen to the adult's position.

5. Come to an agreement.

Lesson 19. Responding to Requests from Parents, Teachers, and Employers

⊟ **Negative Example**

Narrator: Todd has a part-time evening job at his neighborhood gas station. Todd's employer allows him to study when he is not busy waiting on customers or when things are slow. He works from 6:00 to 10:00 p.m. Monday through Thursday. Todd is doing his math assignment at the counter. It's homework that he could have done earlier in the afternoon, but Todd had played basketball after school rather than doing his math assignment and getting ready for work. He is hurrying to get done so he can finish closing the station. Mr. Vincent, the owner, appears at the door of the station.

Mr. Vincent: Todd, I have a special job for you tonight before you close up.

Narrator: Todd keeps working as if he didn't hear Mr. Vincent.

Mr. Vincent: Todd! Did you hear me?

Todd: Uhhh. Wait a minute will you? I've just got two more problems to do. (keeps working)

Mr. Vincent: Todd, you need to put that away and listen. This is important.

Todd: (impatiently) This is math homework. I can do it and listen to you at the same time.

Mr. Vincent: (getting angry) Todd, put that work away! I have to show you how to do this job!

Todd: (shouting) Hey! You told me I could study on this job. Now you want me to jump whenever you come in. Make up your mind! (throws math book across room)

Mr. Vincent: I'm in a hurry. But if your school work is that important, maybe you had better go home to work on it. You don't have to come in tomorrow night, either. I'm sure you're much too busy to work here!

Todd: That's all right with me! I can't work for a liar anyway! (slams the door on his way out)

⊞ **Positive Example**

Narrator: Todd is working on his math assignment, which is due the next morning. It is 9:30 p.m., a half-hour before closing. Mr. Vincent, Todd's employer, suddenly appears at the door.

Mr. Vincent: Todd, I have a job for you to do before you close tonight.

Todd: (looking up from his homework) Can you wait a minute, please? I have just two problems left to do.

Mr. Vincent: I'm in a real hurry, Todd. This has to be ready tonight so we can finish the job we're doing on Mrs. Curry's car in the morning.

Todd: OK. I can get back to this work later. What do you want me to do?

Mr. Vincent: Thanks, Todd. This is real important. Come out to the rack and I'll show you. (Both leave the room and move to the lube rack.)

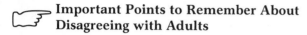 **Important Points to Remember About Responding to Requests from Parents, Teachers, and Employers**

1. Answer right away when an adult speaks to you.

2. Answer politely.

3. If you have a problem with a request, use the skill of disagreeing with adults. (*Exception:* Point #3 *does not* apply if you are requested to do something that you know or feel is wrong or dangerous. In that case, *refuse, leave, and get help immediately.*)

4. If you don't have a problem with the request, do it right away.

62

EXERCISE 1

Narrator: Keith is watching an exciting movie on TV. His mom is getting his little brother and sister ready for bed. The phone rings.

Mom: Keith?!

Keith: (ignores – no response)

Mom: Keith! Would you get that? I have the kids in the bathtub!

Keith: (angrily) Oh, Mom! It's the best part of the movie!

Mom: Keith, please! You always seem to have an excuse.

Keith: OK, I'll get it! (answers the phone)

✔ Checklist For Exercise 1

Did Keith . . .	Yes	No
1. Answer right away?	☐	☐
2. Answer politely?	☐	☐
3. Have a problem with the request and use the skill of disagreeing with adults?	☐	☐
4. Do what his mom asked right away?	☐	☐

EXERCISE 2

Narrator: Emily is baby-sitting for her Aunt Ruth.

Aunt Ruth: I'll be gone about 4 hours. Please do the lunch dishes and straighten up the house while I'm gone.

Emily: Excuse me, Aunt Ruth, but I may not be able to do that if the kids play outside. I feel that I should be out with them, in case they need me.

Aunt Ruth: Well, the baby should take a nap and I'd like Zack to rest inside for about an hour, too.

Emily: OK, then I should be able to get the kitchen cleaned up.

Aunt Ruth: Great. Of course, I plan to pay you extra for that.

Emily: Thanks, Aunt Ruth.

✔ Checklist For Exercise 2

Did Emily . . .	Yes	No
1. Answer right away?	☐	☐
2. Answer politely?	☐	☐
3. Have a problem with her aunt's request and use the skill of disagreeing with an adult?	☐	☐
4. Do what her aunt asked right away?	☐	☐

EXERCISE 3

Narrator: Richard and David are discussing their plans for the weekend before class starts.

Ms. Howe: Excuse me, boys, could you please go to your seats? I'd like to read the announcements a little early today so we have plenty of time for the test.

David: Sure.

Richard: No problem.

Narrator: Boys stop talking and go to their seats.

✔ Checklist For Exercise 3

Did Richard and David . . .	Yes	No
1. Answer right away?	☐	☐
2. Answer politely?	☐	☐
3. Have a problem with the teacher's request and use the skill of disagreeing with adults?	☐	☐
4. Do what the teacher asked right away?	☐	☐

★ Situational Role Play Evaluation Guidelines

	Situational Role Play				
	#1	#2	#3	#4	#5
1. Answer right away.	—	—	—	—	—
2. Answer politely.	—	—	—	—	—

3. If you have a problem with an adult request, use the skill of disagreeing with adults. (*Exception:* If you are requested to do something that is wrong or dangerous, *refuse, leave, and get help immediately.*)   — — — — —

4. If you don't have a problem with the request, do it right away.   — — — — —

Apply the Triple A Strategy   — — — — —

Lesson 19
Student Contract

Directions: Fill in the blanks with the appropriate answers and check with the teacher.

In what situation will you use the skill of responding to adult requests?

_____

_____

_____

What do you think might happen if you don't use the skill of responding to adult requests in this situation?

_____

_____

_____

With whom will you use this skill?

_____

_____

_____

What do you expect to happen when you use the skill of responding to adult requests?

_____

_____

_____

I agree to try this skill with all its important points by (date) _____ . I will do my best to respond appropriately to requests made by adults I know, and I will report back to my class accurately and truthfully about how I used this skill and what the outcomes were.

_____   _____
Signed by student   Signed by teacher

LESSON 20. DOING QUALITY WORK

Review of Lesson 19 (Responding to Requests from Parents, Teachers, and Employers)

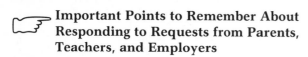 **Important Points to Remember About Responding to Requests from Parents, Teachers, and Employers**

1. Answer right away.

2. Answer politely.

3. If you have a problem with a request, use the skill of disagreeing with adults. (*Exception:* If you are requested to do something that is wrong or dangerous, *refuse, leave, and get help immediately.*)

4. If you don't have a problem with the request, do it right away.

Lesson 20. Doing Quality Work

⊟ Negative Example

Narrator: Gretchen has a job as a motel maid for the summer. The head maid, Alice, checks each room after Gretchen cleans it.

Alice: I spent 15 minutes doing Room 311 over for you.

Gretchen: Huh? What was wrong with it?

Alice: The shower wasn't dry, the bedspread wasn't on straight, you forgot to put stationery in the drawer, and there was a sock under the bed.

Gretchen: Stationery? I didn't know I was supposed to check stationery! And the shower was clean. It would have dried by itself. Picky, picky, picky!

Alice: It sounds picky but that's why this is an expensive motel. Guests expect everything to be perfect. If you can't handle that, maybe this isn't the job for you.

⊞ Positive Example

Alice: Your work has really improved during the last week or so. What happened, Gretchen?

Gretchen: Well, it helps to have that list of everything we're supposed to do right on my cart. I check it before I go into the room, a couple of times while I'm working, and before I leave to make sure I've done everything.

Alice: That's great, but that doesn't explain why you're doing so much better making beds and folding towels and things like that.

Gretchen: Well, I took a look at the way you and some of the other maids make beds, and I finally saw how much better your rooms looked than mine. And I figured, this is a nice place and if I want to work here I'd better come up to your standards. It feels good to know the room is perfect when I'm done with it.

Alice: Well, 311 must have been perfect. The guest left a nice note and a good tip for you.

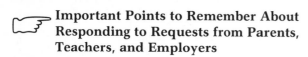 **Important Points to Remember About Doing Quality Work**

1. Understand what to do before you begin.

2. Do work that is neat, complete, and up to standard.

3. Check your work; be willing to do it over if necessary.

EXERCISE 1

Narrator: Sara and Kay are the last ones in the pizza parlor where they work. They are closing up for the night.

Sara: Come on! Let's get out of here. It's creepy here at this time of night.

Kay: I'm almost done. Help me finish loading the dishwasher and check the list and see what else we're supposed to do before we leave.

Sara: Oh, forget it. I'm leaving. You coming with me?

Kay: Well, since you're driving, I guess I'm leaving, too.

✔ Checklist For Exercise 1

Did Sara and Kay . . .	Yes	No
1. Understand what to do before they began?	☐	☐
2. Do work that was neat, complete, and up to standard?	☐	☐

3. Check their work; do it over if necessary? ☐ ☐

EXERCISE 2

Narrator: Ken is working in study hall. His friend Seth comes over to talk to him.

Seth: What are you doing?

Ken: Checking over my report for Smith's class.

Seth: Oh, that. Boy, you really wrote a lot. I only wrote one page single spaced.

Ken: It's supposed to be double spaced and 500 words. You can't get that on one page.

Seth: (shrugs) Well, hurry up and then help me with my math.

Ken: Nope. I have to copy this over.

Seth: Are you kidding? You're going to do it again? Why?

Ken: I want to change a few things, clean it up a little.

Seth: I can't believe this!

Ken: Yeah, well, what kind of grade are *you* getting in that class?

Seth: Never mind. See you later.

✔ Checklist For Exercise 2

Did Ken . . .   **Yes**   **No**

1. Understand what to do before he began? ☐ ☐

2. Do work that was neat, complete, and up to standard? ☐ ☐

3. Check his work; do it over if necessary? ☐ ☐

EXERCISE 3

Narrator: Chip is doing yard work on Saturday morning while his parents run errands. His friend Phil comes by.

Phil: How much longer do you have to work, Chip? I was wondering if you wanted to go on a bike ride with me.

Chip: Yeah, I'd like to. I'm supposed to rake after I finish mowing, but Dad will never notice if I skip it. Be with you in a couple minutes.

✔ Checklist For Exercise 3

Did Chip . . .   **Yes**   **No**

1. Understand what to do before he began? ☐ ☐

2. Do work that was neat, complete, and up to standard? ☐ ☐

3. Check his work; do it over if necessary? ☐ ☐

★ Situational Role Play Evaluation Guidelines

	Situational Role Play				
	#1	#2	#3	#4	#5
1. Understand what to do before you begin.	—	—	—	—	—
2. Do work that is neat, complete, and up to standard.	—	—	—	—	—
3. Check your work, be willing to do it over if necessary.	—	—	—	—	—
Apply the Triple A Strategy	—	—	—	—	—

Lesson 20
Student Contract

Directions: Fill in the blanks with the appropriate answers and check with the teacher.

In what situation will you use the skill of doing quality work?

_____

_____

_____

What might happen if you didn't use this skill in this situation?

_____

_____

_____

What people will be affected when you use this skill?

_____

_____

_____

What do you expect to happen when you use the skill of doing quality work in this situation?

_____

_____

_____

I agree to try this skill with all its important points by (date) _____ . I will do my best to do quality work, and I will report back to my class accurately and truthfully about how I used this skill and what the outcomes were.

_____   _____
Signed by student   Signed by teacher

LESSON 21. WORKING INDEPENDENTLY

Review of Lesson 20 (Doing Quality Work)

☞ **Important Points to Remember About Doing Quality Work**

1. Understand what to do before you begin.

2. Do work that is neat, complete, and up to standard.

3. Check your work; be willing to do it over if necessary.

Lesson 21. Working Independently

⊟ **Negative Example**

Narrator: Kim's boss is telling his workers to get ready for a big rush in the restaurant because it's prom night. Kim is constantly distracted, looking at all the couples as they come in and gossiping with the other waitresses and waiters about the customers. She is describing one of the couples to another waitress in the kitchen when her boss comes up to her.

Boss: Kim, get to work please.

Kim: Sure, what do you want me to do?

Boss: (impatiently) We went over that this afternoon. Get the tables cleared as fast as you can. All our tables are reserved all evening. And Kim, when you clear the tables, please be sure they are *clean*. Sometimes you're not too careful about that.

Kim: OK, sure. But I just remembered, I can't start working yet because I can't find my order pad. What should I do?

Boss: (exasperated) Get another one! Write on a piece of paper! Whatever! Just get to work!

Kim: OK, OK!

Narrator: The boss leaves looking very irritated.

⊞ **Positive Example**

Boss: All our tables are reserved all night. That means we have to keep things moving. Don't rush people, but don't waste any time bringing the check or menu or getting the tables cleared.

Narrator: Kim listens closely as her boss speaks, gets out her pen and order pad, and ignores the person beside her who is trying to tell her about one of the couples in the restaurant. She starts working. Later she passes her boss on the way to the kitchen with a tray of dirty dishes.

Kim: Mr. Dawes, could I speak to you when you have a minute?

Boss: I'm busy now. I'll get back to you.

Narrator: A few minutes later Mr. Dawes finds Kim setting a table.

Boss: What is it, Kim?

Kim: My order pad is empty. I've been writing on scraps of paper, but I don't think the cook likes it. I don't have time to see if there's one in the employees' room.

Boss: You keep working. I'll get you one. You're really doing a great job of working fast, but still doing the job well.

Kim: Thank you. The customers seem to think so, too. The tips are great tonight!

☞ **Important Points to Remember About Working Independently**

1. Do quality work (see review list of important points at beginning of this lesson).

2. Try to figure things out for yourself.

3. Ask for help when you need it, but keep working while you wait.

4. Have the materials you need.

5. Stay on task.

EXERCISE 1

Narrator: Eric is in social studies class, and the teacher is giving an assignment.

Teacher: Read the article and list five problems facing China today.

Narrator: Eric starts reading, then raises hand and stops reading.

Eric: What are we supposed to do?

Teacher: Read the article and jot down five problems China has.

Eric: (reads for a moment) Do we have to read the whole article or just stop when we find five?

Teacher: Read the whole thing.

Eric: (reads for a minute, then raises hand) Do these have to be complete sentences?

Teacher: No, Eric, just read it and jot them down.

Narrator: Eric finally settles down and reads the article.

✔ Checklist For Exercise 1

Did Eric . . .   **Yes**   **No**

1. Do quality work?   ☐   ☐

2. Try to figure things out for himself?   ☐   ☐

3. Ask for help when needed, but keep
   working while he waited?   ☐   ☐

4. Have the materials he needed?   ☐   ☐

5. Stay on task?   ☐   ☐

EXERCISE 2

Narrator: Carol and Judy work for Briggs Yard Maintenance. Mr. Briggs told them to weed the flower beds in the yard they are working on.

Carol: (sitting down to rest) Why didn't you pull that one out?

Judy: Because it's not a weed, you dope.

Carol: It's not? I've pulled out dozens of them!

Judy: Didn't you watch when Mr. Briggs told us what to do?

Carol: No. Boy, my hands are sore.

Judy: That's what you get for forgetting your gloves. Are you about ready to get back to work?

Carol: Don't rush me. Briggs is nowhere around. I'll just wait til he comes and yells at me to get to work.

✔ Checklist For Exercise 2

Did Carol . . .   **Yes**   **No**

1. Do quality work?   ☐   ☐

2. Try to figure things out for herself?   ☐   ☐

3. Ask for help when needed, but keep
   working while she waited?   ☐   ☐

4. Have the materials she needed?   ☐   ☐

5. Stay on task?   ☐   ☐

EXERCISE 3

Narrator: The Sterge family is doing Saturday morning chores.

Andy: I finished sweeping the garage. What are you working on?

Bobby: Just finished mowing and now I have to rake.

Andy: OK, I'll help. Are we supposed to water after that?

Bobby: I don't know. I'll go ask Dad.

Andy: No you don't! Keep working. We can ask him when he comes outside. Let's get this done and maybe we can get to the track meet in time for the steeplechase, for a change.

Bobby: You're right. Grab that rake.

✔ Checklist For Exercise 3

Did Andy and Bobby . . .   **Yes**   **No**

1. Do quality work?   ☐   ☐

2. Try to figure things out for
   themselves?   ☐   ☐

3. Ask for help when needed, but keep
   working while they waited?   ☐   ☐

4. Have the materials they needed?   ☐   ☐

5. Stay on task?   ☐   ☐

★ Situational Role Play Evaluation Guidelines

	Situational Role Play				
	#1	**#2**	**#3**	**#4**	**#5**
1. Do quality work.	—	—	—	—	—
2. Try to figure things out for yourself.	—	—	—	—	—
3. Ask for help when you need it, but keep working while you wait.	—	—	—	—	—
4. Have the materials you need.	—	—	—	—	—
5. Stay on task.	—	—	—	—	—
Apply the Triple A Strategy	—	—	—	—	—

Lesson 21
Student Contract

Directions: Fill in the blanks with the appropriate answers and check with the teacher.

In what situation will you use the skill of working independently?

_____

_____

_____

What might happen if you didn't use this skill in that situation?

_____

_____

_____

What adults will be involved when you use this skill?

_____

_____

_____

What do you expect to happen when you use the skill of working independently?

_____

_____

_____

I agree to try to use the skill of working independently with all its important points by (date) _____ . I will do my best to work independently, and I will report back to my class accurately and truthfully about how I used this skill and what the outcomes were.

_____   _____
Signed by student   Signed by teacher

LESSON 22. DEVELOPING GOOD WORK HABITS

Review of Lesson 21 (Working Independently)

☞ Important Points to Remember About Working Independently

1. Do quality work.

2. Try to figure things out for yourself.

3. Ask for help when you need it, but keep working while you wait.

4. Have the materials you need.

5. Stay on task.

Lesson 22. Developing Good Work Habits

⊟ Negative Example

Narrator: Emily has a job on a park maintenance crew. She is wandering around the tool shed area looking as if she's daydreaming when Joe approaches.

Joe: Hey, Em! We've been waiting for you! Where have you been?

Emily: I guess I was a little late this morning and now I can't find the tools I need.

Joe: Don't you remember? The boss took all the tools out for us earlier this morning. He told us that when we finished last night.

Emily: Oh, yeah. I forgot. I'll be right there.

Narrator: Emily goes with the crew to the park. When they arrive, she gets her tools and starts looking for the hedges she is supposed to trim. On her way, she stops to talk with a boy she knows. Twenty minutes later she finds the hedges and starts to work. After about 10 minutes of clipping, Emily is thirsty so she goes off to look for a water fountain. On the way she stops to talk with Joe, who keeps working while Emily watches and talks. Mr. Boyer, the boss, comes over.

Mr. Boyer: Emily, I've been watching you. It's almost lunch time and you have worked only about 10 minutes. Do you have some problem with this job?

Emily: Oh, no! I really like the job. It's fun and the crew is great. I'll really work hard this afternoon. I promise. (Mr. Boyer leaves.)

Emily: (to Joe) How do you like that! He's making a big deal about one ratty hedge in this crummy park. What's *he* doing besides spying on me?

Joe: It's his job to make sure you work, Emily.

Emily: Hey, I'm entitled to breaks, you know!

Joe: Some break! Eight to noon!

⊞ Positive Example

Narrator: Emily arrives at work on time, quickly gets the tools she needs, and gets started on her assigned work. After a couple of hours, Joe comes over.

Joe: Break time, Emily.

Emily: I'm working through break today. I asked Mr. Boyer if I could leave early to go to the dentist and he said OK. I thought that was really nice of him, considering how much work we have to do today.

Dan: Did he say you have to skip break?

Emily: No, but I want to get this weeding done here this afternoon. We won't be back in this park for 2 weeks.

Dan: I know. It's really going to look good when we get done, isn't it?

Emily: Yeah, this park department does a pretty good job, considering they don't have much money to spend. Enjoy your break. Could you come over here afterward and help me trim those high branches? I can't quite reach them.

Joe: Sure. Be back in 10 minutes.

☞ Important Points to Remember About Developing Good Work Habits

1. Work a full shift.

2. Do quality work.

   Important points to remember for doing quality work:
   a. Understand what to do before you begin.

b. Do work that is neat, complete, and up to standard.

c. Check your work; be willing to do it over if necessary.

3. Work independently (see review list of important points at beginning of this lesson).

4. Get along with others.

5. Speak well of your employer.

EXERCISE 1

Narrator: Russell has a job in a greenhouse. He works hard, gets the job done, and requires minimal supervision. Russell likes everything about his job except the other kid who works there, Sheldon.

Sheldon: What's happening, Russ?

Russell: I've told you a hundred times, the name is Russell.

Sheldon: Well, excuse me. Ready for break?

Russell: Not with you. I'm going to check those orchids you just watered. They look pretty sick.

Sheldon: Are you saying I'm not doing my job? Do you want to go with me to the boss to discuss it?

(Russell walks away, ignoring Sheldon.)

✔ Checklist For Exercise 1

Did Russell . . .   Yes   No

1. Work a full shift?   ☐   ☐

2. Do quality work?   ☐   ☐

3. Work independently?   ☐   ☐

4. Get along with others?   ☐   ☐

5. Speak well of his employer?   ☐   ☐

EXERCISE 2

Narrator: In the summer Courtney works in a roadside fruit and vegetable stand. Today she's working with a new girl, Melissa.

Melissa: What do we do when we don't have any customers?

Courtney: I rearrange the stuff, take out the berries that look a little shriveled, polish the apples, stuff like that.

Melissa: If we don't have any customers, can we close early?

Courtney: I'm tempted sometimes, but we always get a lot of people stopping on their way home from work, so we have to stay open. Here comes one now. Hello, sir.

Customer: Hi. Is the corn fresh?

Courtney: Just picked about 2 hours ago. I'd like to recommend the raspberries, too. It's a great crop this year.

Customer: Okay, a dozen ears of corn and a quart of raspberries.

✔ Checklist For Exercise 2

Did Courtney . . .   Yes   No

1. Work a full shift?   ☐   ☐

2. Do quality work?   ☐   ☐

3. Work independently?   ☐   ☐

4. Get along with others?   ☐   ☐

5. Speak well of her employer?   ☐   ☐

EXERCISE 3

Narrator: Meredith works at Hailey's Ice Cream Parlor. She loves ice cream, but she has always thought Bridges's ice cream was better than Hailey's.

Kristen: Meredith! What are you doing here? I never thought you'd work at Hailey's.

Meredith: (shrugs) It's a job, I guess.

Kristen: I thought you didn't like Hailey's ice cream. You always made such a big deal of it.

Meredith: I don't like it. If you were smart you would go across the street to Bridges's.

✔ Checklist For Exercise 3

Did Meredith . . .   **Yes**   **No**

1. Work a full shift?   ☐   ☐

2. Do quality work?   ☐   ☐

3. Work independently?   ☐   ☐

4. Get along with others?   ☐   ☐

5. Speak well of her employer?   ☐   ☐

★ Situational Role Play Evaluation Guidelines

	#1	**#2**	**#3**	**#4**	**#5**
Situational Role Play					
1. Work a full shift.	—	—	—	—	—
2. Do quality work.	—	—	—	—	—
3. Work independently.	—	—	—	—	—
4. Get along with others.	—	—	—	—	—
5. Speak well of your employer.	—	—	—	—	—
Apply the Triple A Strategy	—	—	—	—	—

Lesson 22
Student Contract

Directions: Fill in the blanks with the appropriate answers and check with the teacher.

In what situation will you use the skill of developing good work habits?

_____

_____

_____

What do you think might happen if you didn't use this skill in the situation you described?

_____

_____

_____

Who will be affected when you use this skill?

_____

_____

_____

What do you expect to happen when you use this skill?

_____

_____

_____

I agree to try this skill with all its important points by (date) _____ . I will do my best to develop good work habits, and I will report back to my class accurately and truthfully about how I used this skill and what the outcomes were.

_____   _____
Signed by student   Signed by teacher

LESSON 23. FOLLOWING CLASSROOM RULES

Review of Lesson 22 (Developing Good Work Habits)

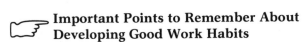 **Important Points to Remember About Developing Good Work Habits**

1. Work a full shift.

2. Do quality work.

3. Work independently.

4. Get along with others.

5. Speak well of your employer.

Lesson 23. Following Classroom Rules

⊟ **Negative Example**

Narrator: Randy is in class listening to his Walkman. His teacher seems to be annoyed about that.

Mr. Biggs: Randy, put the tape player away, please. No stereos in class.

(Randy doesn't hear, doesn't answer.)

Mr. Biggs: (louder) Randy, put that stereo away!

Randy: Aw, come on. I can study and listen at the same time.

Mr. Biggs: It's a school policy, no tape players except between classes.

Randy: Well, Mr. Crosby lets us have them in class. It helps me concentrate.

Mr. Biggs: Please put it away or I'll take it away from you.

Randy: OK, OK, what a tyrant!

⊞ **Positive Example**

Mr. Biggs: Randy, put the tape player away, please. No tape players in class.

Randy: Oh, yeah, I forgot. Mr. Crosby lets us have them and I just got used to studying with it. Sorry. (puts stereo away)

☞ **REVIEW: Important Points to Remember About Responding to Requests by Parents, Teachers, and Employers**

1. Answer right away when an adult speaks to you.

2. Answer politely.

3. If you have a problem with a request, use the skill of disagreeing with adults.

4. If you don't have a problem with the request, do it right away.

☞ **Important Points to Remember About Following Classroom Rules**

1. Know the school rules and the rules for each class.

2. Follow the rules.

3. Help others follow the rules.

4. If you break a rule, accept the consequences.

5. If you have a serious problem with a rule, follow the steps for disagreeing with adults.

☞ **REVIEW: Important Points to Remember About Disagreeing with Adults**

1. Choose or ask for a good time to talk.

2. Be prepared to tell your side of the problem.

3. Use a calm, respectful tone of voice.

4. Listen to the adult's position.

5. Come to an agreement.

EXERCISE 1

Narrator: Dan is tardy to class.

Teacher: Dan, we're taking a quiz. Just pick up where we are and I'll repeat the ones you missed later.

Dan: Can I borrow a pencil?

Teacher: (exasperated) You don't have a pencil? You know you are supposed to have the materials you need every day. That's a classroom rule.

Dan: Well, I don't have a pencil so what are you going to do about it?

Teacher: I'm not going to hold up the rest of the class while we argue about it. Let's continue with the quiz.

Dan: Well, if I can't take the quiz I might as well leave.

Teacher: You won't get credit for today if you can't do the work so you might as well go to the office.

✔ Checklist For Exercise 1

Did Dan . . .   Yes   No

1. Know the rules for this classroom?   ☐   ☐

2. Follow the rules?   ☐   ☐

3. Help others follow the rules?   ☐   ☐

4. Accept the consequences for breaking a rule?   ☐   ☐

5. Have a serious problem with a rule and follow the steps for disagreeing with adults?   ☐   ☐

EXERCISE 2

Narrator: Rick is on his way to electronics class with his friend Ron.

Rick: Oh no!

Ron: What's up?

Rick: I just remembered I can't wear sandals to electronics class.

Ron: Why not? That seems like a dumb rule.

Rick: Oh, it's a safety thing. If you drop the hot solder on your foot it causes a real serious burn. Anyway, I'm going to run down to my P.E. locker and get my gym shoes. See you later.

✔ Checklist For Exercise 2

Did Rick . . .   Yes   No

1. Know the rules for this class?   ☐   ☐

2. Follow the rules?   ☐   ☐

3. Help others follow the rules?   ☐   ☐

4. Accept the consequences for breaking a rule?   ☐   ☐

5. Have a serious problem with a rule and follow the steps for disagreeing with adults?   ☐   ☐

EXERCISE 3

Narrator: Sam and Lon walk into class wearing baseball caps.

Teacher: The caps will have to go, fellas.

Sam: Aw, today's the big game against South. Can't we wear them just today?

Teacher: It's school policy. Sorry.

Sam: Gimme a break. What's the big deal? Who does it bother if I wear a baseball cap?

Lon: Easy, Sam, let's just take them off. No big deal. We can put them back on after class.

Narrator: Sam and Lon remove caps.

✔ Checklist For Exercise 3

Did Sam and Lon . . .   Yes   No

1. Know the rules for this class?   ☐   ☐

2. Follow the rules?   ☐   ☐

3. Help others follow the rules?   ☐   ☐

4. Accept the consequences for breaking a rule?   ☐   ☐

5. Have a serious problem with a rule and follow the steps for disagreeing with adults?   ☐   ☐

★ Situational Role Play Evaluation Guidelines

	Situational Role Play				
	#1	#2	#3	#4	#5
1. Know the school rules and rules for each class.	—	—	—	—	—
2. Follow the rules.	—	—	—	—	—

3. Help others follow the
   rules.   — — — — —

4. If you break a rule, accept
   the consequences.   — — — — —

5. If you have a serious
   problem with a rule, follow the steps for disagreeing with adults.   — — — — —

Apply the Triple A Strategy   — — — — —

Lesson 23
Student Contract

Directions: Fill in the blanks with appropriate answers and check with the teacher.

In what situation will you use the skill of following classroom rules?

_____

_____

With what teacher will you use this skill?

_____

_____

What are the rules in this teacher's classroom?

_____

_____

What do you think might happen if you didn't use this skill in this situation?

_____

_____

What do you expect to happen when you use this skill in this situation?

_____

_____

I agree to try this skill with all its important points by (date) _____ . I will do my best to follow classroom rules, and I will report back to my class accurately and truthfully about how I used this skill and what the outcomes were.

_____   _____
Signed by student   Signed by teacher

LESSON 24. DEVELOPING GOOD STUDY HABITS

Review of Lesson 23 (Following Classroom Rules)

☞ **Important Points to Remember About Following Classroom Rules**

1. Know the school rules and the rules for each class.

2. Follow the rules.

3. Help others follow the rules.

4. If you break a rule, accept the consequences.

5. If you have a serious problem with a rule, follow the steps for disagreeing with adults.

Lesson 24. Developing Good Study Habits

⊟ **Negative Example**

Narrator: Ken is wearing a Walkman stereo and is sprawled on the floor watching TV. Books and papers are scattered everywhere. The phone rings.

Ken: Hi, Jeff. What's up? Hey, me too. I've got so much homework: the math test, a bunch of questions in government, and a whole pile of pages to read in that English book. (pause) No, the math test isn't over that stuff. I think it's chapter 9. (pause) Are you sure? I don't know what to study for now. Wait a minute. Well, I can't find my math book anyway. I guess I left it in my locker. One less thing to do!

⊞ **Positive Example**

Narrator: Ken is in a quiet room, with no TV or radio, and with his materials organized. He checks his assignment notebook. The phone rings.

Ken: Hi, Jeff. I can't talk long right now. I've got a ton of homework. You too? That's right; the math test is over chapter 10. Well, for government I'm going to skim through the chapter first, and then read through the questions at the end. Then I'll read the chapter again carefully, study it to try to answer the questions, and then test myself over what I read. Yeah, that really works well for me. Hey, I have to get started now. See you later.

☞ **Important Points to Remember About Developing Good Study Habits**

1. Keep track of materials and assignments.

2. Have a regular time and place to study.

3. Learn a good study system.

4. Allow enough time for each assignment.

5. Ask for and complete make-up work.

___

EXERCISE 1

Narrator: Mike is working at his desk. His materials are well organized, outlined, and there are no distractions. He looks at the clock.

Mike: Only 15 minutes to get this math done and read half a chapter! I'd better get going if I want to get done in time to see Monday Night Football.

✔ **Checklist For Exercise 1**

Did Mike . . .	Yes	No
1. Keep track of materials and assignments?	☐	☐
2. Have a regular time and place to study?	☐	☐
3. Learn a good study system?	☐	☐
4. Allow enough time for each assignment?	☐	☐
5. Ask for and complete make-up work?	☐	☐

___

EXERCISE 2

Narrator: Kate is studying math at her desk in her bedroom. The phone rings.

Kate: Hi, Beth. No, I haven't started my history assignment yet. I'm doing things in order – math first, because I was absent last week and have to get caught up. I'll call you back when I get done in about 15 minutes and then we can figure it out together, OK?

✔ **Checklist For Exercise 2**

Did Kate . . .   Yes   No

1. Keep track of materials and assignments?   ☐   ☐

2. Have a regular time and place to study?   ☐   ☐

3. Learn a good study system?   ☐   ☐

4. Allow enough time for each assignment?   ☐   ☐

5. Ask for, and complete make-up work?   ☐   ☐

EXERCISE 3

Narrator: Lisa has been reading her history book every afternoon at the living room table. She has given herself plenty of time to go over the chapters for the exam and has kept all her homework assignments in order. Still, when her sister comes into the room, she is frustrated.

Lisa: I give up! I've been staring at this book for hours and I still don't know a thing about the World War I. I can't believe it!

Kelly: Well, tell me how you study it.

Lisa: I just read it and try to memorize it.

Kelly: Memorize a whole history book? No wonder you're not getting anything out of it.

✔ **Checklist For Exercise 3**

Did Lisa . . .   Yes   No

1. Keep track of materials and assignments?   ☐   ☐

2. Have a regular time and place to study?   ☐   ☐

3. Learn a good study system?   ☐   ☐

4. Allow enough time for each assignment?   ☐   ☐

5. Ask for and complete make-up work?   ☐   ☐

★ **Situational Role Play Evaluation Guidelines**

	Situational Role Play				
	#1	#2	#3	#4	#5
1. Keep track of materials and assignments.	—	—	—	—	—
2. Have a regular time and place to study.	—	—	—	—	—
3. Learn a good study system.	—	—	—	—	—
4. Allow enough time for each assignment.	—	—	—	—	—
5. Ask for and complete make-up work.	—	—	—	—	—
Apply the Triple A Strategy	—	—	—	—	—

Lesson 24
Student Contract

Directions: Fill in the blanks with the appropriate answers and check with your teacher.

In what situation will you use the skill of developing good study habits?

_____

_____

What do you think might happen if you don't use this skill in that situation?

_____

_____

Where will you use this skill?

_____

_____

What changes do you need to make in order to have good study habits?

_____

_____

What people will be affected if you make those changes?

_____

_____

What do you expect to happen when you use this skill?

_____

_____

I agree to try this skill with all its important points by (date) _____ . I will do my best to develop good study habits and I will report back to my class accurately and truthfully about how I used this skill and what the outcomes were.

_____   _____
Signed by student   Signed by teacher

LESSON 25. TAKING PRIDE IN YOUR APPEARANCE

Review of Lesson 24 (Developing Good Study Habits)

👉 **Important Points to Remember About Developing Good Study Habits**

1. Keep track of materials and assignments.

2. Have a regular time and place to study.

3. Learn a good study system.

4. Allow enough time for each assignment.

5. Ask for and complete make-up work.

Lesson 25. Taking Pride in Your Appearance

➖ **Negative Example**

Narrator: Julie, Karen, and Ross are scheduled to work the noon hour in the school store.

Julie: Hey, Karen, here I am! Who else is scheduled to work today?

Karen: My favorite and yours, Mr. Sloth himself.

Julie: Oh *no*! Not Ross! I don't think I can stand to be in the same booth with him. He has the worst B.O. Not to mention his breath. *Nobody* will buy anything from us.

Karen: No kidding, you should see him today! Black, I mean *black* fingernails; his shirt looks and smells like a dog bed and the zipper on his pants is broken. Maybe we can get him to work in the back.

Julie: Oh, barf. When Mr. Anderson hired us he did say we had to look reasonably nice. How did Ross get this job anyway?

Karen: I think Mr. Anderson felt sorry for him – poverty case or something.

Julie: Well, maybe he doesn't have much money, but really, soap is cheap!

Karen: I think he just doesn't care. My brother says he never even showers after P.E. The guy's a loser.

Ross: (enters) Hey, you two, I was right outside the door and heard every word you said about me!

Karen: Well, Ross, maybe it's time you did hear.

Ross: Yeah? Well, that hurts. I quit!

➕ **Positive Example**

Julie: Hi, Karen, who else is working today?

Karen: Ross Johnson. He'll be here in just a minute.

Julie: Oh good! I really like being around Ross. He sure knows how to take care of himself and it shows.

Karen: I'm glad Mr. Anderson hired him to work on our shift.

Julie: Me, too. You know, Ross sets a great example and, of course, we never have trouble selling a thing when he works here. He always looks neat and clean.

Karen: Yeah, it's funny. Ross doesn't have the most expensive clothes or anything, but he looks good. My brother told me Ross works out *every* day after school!

Ross: (enters) Well, if it isn't Julie and Karen. How are you guys doing?

Julie: Fine. Would you like to work up front today?

👉 **Important Points to Remember About Taking Pride in Your Appearance**

1. Pay attention to how you look and feel.

2. Make health and hygiene care a regular habit.

3. Maintain your clothing and appearance.

4. Dress for the occasion.

EXERCISE 1

Jack: Hey Spaceman, where did you find that get up? On Mars? This is, you know, *school*.

Dean: Yeah, I guess it looks pretty stupid. I was in a hurry and just threw this on.

Jack: Looks like you just "threw it on" all right. Your shirt is inside out and it looks like you missed on those socks again, eh Dean? Hip is one thing, ridiculous is another.

Dean: Come on, Jack, I feel bad enough.

Jack: You feel bad? Well, I got some news, you look bad too.

Dean: Doesn't look that bad, does it?

Jack: If today were Halloween, I might agree. I'm checking out of here before someone starts associating you with me!

✔ Checklist For Exercise 1

Did Dean . . .	Yes	No
1. Pay attention to how he looks and feels?	☐	☐
2. Make health and hygiene care a regular habit?	☐	☐
3. Maintain his clothing and appearance?	☐	☐
4. Dress for the occasion?	☐	☐

EXERCISE 2

MiMi: Carolyn, what are you doing wolfing down all those carbos? You're supposed to be getting ready to go skating with me. You're not wearing that, are you?

Carolyn: I like this muumuu! But I can see you don't, so I'm not going!

MiMi: Why not? This is the third time you've canceled out on me. Besides, I think you could use the exercise. Just change, you can't skate in a muumuu.

Carolyn: I can't fit into any of my clothes; they're all too tight. Besides, I *hate* exercising. I'm not going.

MiMi: Carolyn, you'd feel a lot better about yourself if you'd quit eating all that junk and start exercising for a change.

Carolyn: Just go on without me, OK?

✔ Checklist For Exercise 2

Did Carolyn . . .	Yes	No
1. Pay attention to how she looks and feels?	☐	☐
2. Make health (and hygiene care) a regular habit?	☐	☐
3. Maintain her clothing and appearance?	☐	☐
4. Dress for the occasion?	☐	☐

EXERCISE 3

Tracy: Hey Valerie, wow, you sure did a great job doing that campaign speech for Terry. I'm sure Terry appreciated your style. It sounded great and you looked like a real pro! Where did you get your new haircut? It just looks perfect on you.

Valerie: Well, thanks Tracy. I picked the haircut from a magazine picture. But it did take me forever to get ready! Seems like I tried on all my clothes a thousand times. I really was nervous about getting up in front of everybody. But I think it went OK.

Tracy: No doubt about that. You must have really practiced that speech; and, like I said, you really looked the part up there.

Valerie: Did I ever practice that speech! Every morning out on my bicycle for 2 weeks.

Tracy: What a great idea! I really could learn a few things from you, Val.

✔ Checklist For Exercise 3

Did Valerie . . .	Yes	No
1. Pay attention to how she looks and feels?	☐	☐
2. Make health and hygiene care a regular habit?	☐	☐
3. Maintain her clothing and appearance?	☐	☐
4. Dress for the occasion?	☐	☐

★ Situational Role Play Evaluation Guidelines

	Situational Role Play				
	#1	#2	#3	#4	#5
1. Pay attention to how you look and feel.	—	—	—	—	—
2. Make health and hygiene care a regular habit.	—	—	—	—	—
3. Maintain your clothing and appearance.	—	—	—	—	—
4. Dress for the occasion.	—	—	—	—	—
Apply the Triple A Strategy	—	—	—	—	—

Lesson 25
Student Contract

Directions: Fill in the blanks with the appropriate answers and check with your teacher.

What are some personal goals you have for taking pride in your appearance? (please list)

_____

_____

_____

How will you work on these goals?

_____

_____

_____

What do you expect will happen when you use the skill of taking pride in your appearance as listed above?

_____

_____

_____

What might happen if you didn't use the skill of taking pride in your appearance as listed above?

_____

_____

_____

I agree to try the skill of taking pride in my appearance using the goals I've listed above and its important points by (date) _____ . I will try to do my best to take pride in my appearance, and I will report back to my class accurately and truthfully about how I used this skill and what the outcomes were.

_____   _____
Signed by student   Signed by teacher

LESSON 26. BEING ORGANIZED

Review of Lesson 25 (Taking Pride in Your Appearance)

👉 **Important Points to Remember About Taking Pride in Your Appearance**

1. Pay attention to how you look and feel.

2. Make health and hygiene care a regular habit.

3. Maintain your clothing and appearance.

4. Dress for the occasion.

Lesson 26. Being Organized

⊟ Negative Example

Curtis: Hey, Billy, we better hurry or we'll be late to Mrs. Fitch's class.

Bill: I forgot my watch again. What time is it, anyway?

Curtis: My watch says 2 minutes 'til, come on.

Billy: Two minutes 'til! And I still have to get my stuff from our locker. What's the combination again?

Curtis: Billy, for the 100th time it's 2-2-11! I'll do it. You know, your side of the locker is some trash can. You better move it, we're having that quiz this morning, you know.

Billy: A quiz? You're kidding. What quiz? I went swimming last night. I didn't even take my book home. Do you have an extra pencil?

Curtis: Billy, don't you ever write anything down? I don't see how you could – you never have a pencil. Don't you remember Mrs. Fitch told us about the quiz yesterday? You'll have to find your own pencil this time. I don't want to be late. See you later.

Billy: Some friend you are!

⊞ Positive Example

Curtis: Hey, Billy, how you doing today? Sharing a locker with you is sure OK by me. Your side is always really neat!

Billy: I take care of my side of the locker after school, before the bus comes, so I always know where things are the next day. Hey, look at the time! My watch says 5 minutes 'til. Let's talk on the way to class.

Curtis: Did you do that assignment and study for the quiz?

Billy: Yeah, I think I'm ready for it. I wrote everything down that we were supposed to cover and spent several hours on it last night.

Curtis: You did? I thought you went swimming last night.

Billy: I wanted to, but I got that assignment and had to study instead. I picked up some pencils at the school store this morning. Need one?

Curtis: No thanks. Well, let's ace this quiz.

👉 **Important Points to Remember About Being Organized**

1. Keep track of your belongings.

2. Keep track of your appointments and other responsibilities.

3. Wear a watch.

4. Prioritize things you need to do.

EXERCISE 1

Narrator: Judy is getting dressed for school. Her room is a disaster: piles of clean and dirty clothes, records, tapes, books, dirty dishes, empty cracker boxes, etc.

Mom: Hurry up, Judy, if you want a ride to school. I have to leave for work now.

Judy: I'm not ready! I can't find my other shoe and I want to wear the scarf that goes with this shirt.

Mom: Wear another pair of shoes and forget the scarf, unless you want to walk to school.

Judy: You know I don't have time to walk!

✔ Checklist For Exercise 1

Did Judy . . .	Yes	No
1. Keep track of her belongings?	☐	☐
2. Keep track of her appointments and other responsibilities?	☐	☐

3. Wear a watch? ☐ ☐

4. Prioritize the things she needs to do? ☐ ☐

EXERCISE 2

Greg: What time do you want me to pick you up tomorrow?

Tony: Huh?

Greg: You know, to help me work on my car. You said you'd help me on Saturday.

Tony: Oh, man! I forgot. I told my dad I'd do a bunch of stuff for him tomorrow, too.

Greg: Can you get out of it?

Tony: No way. He already paid me for it and I spent the money.

Greg: Well, that's just great. What am I supposed to do now?

✔ Checklist For Exercise 2

Did Tony . . .   **Yes**   **No**

1. Keep track of his belongings? ☐ ☐

2. Keep track of his appointments and other responsibilities? ☐ ☐

3. Wear a watch? ☐ ☐

4. Prioritize the things he needs to do? ☐ ☐

EXERCISE 3

Narrator: Sue is standing outside a movie theater, looking at her watch. Mary runs up to her.

Mary: Sorry I'm late. I didn't realize it takes so long to get here from my house. Let's go in.

Sue: The movie started 10 minutes ago. I don't want to go in late.

Mary: It can't be that late! What time is it?

Sue: I'll tell you what time it is, it's too late!

✔ Checklist For Exercise 3

Did Mary . . .   **Yes**   **No**

1. Keep track of her belongings? ☐ ☐

2. Keep track of her appointments and other responsibilities? ☐ ☐

3. Wear a watch? ☐ ☐

4. Prioritize the things she needs to do? ☐ ☐

★ Situational Role Play Evaluation Guidelines

	Situational Role Play				
	#1	**#2**	**#3**	**#4**	**#5**
1. Keep track of your belongings.	—	—	—	—	—
2. Keep track of your appointments and other responsibilities.	—	—	—	—	—
3. Wear a watch.	—	—	—	—	—
4. Prioritize the things you need to do.	—	—	—	—	—
Apply the Triple A Strategy	—	—	—	—	—

Lesson 26
Student Contract

Directions: Fill in the blanks with the appropriate answers and check with your teacher.

In what situation will you use the skill of being organized?

_____

_____

_____

What are some problems that might come up if you are not organized in that situation?

_____

_____

_____

Who will be affected if you become more organized in the situation you listed?

_____

_____

_____

What do you expect to happen when you use the skill of being organized in this situation?

_____

_____

_____

I agree to try this skill with all its important points by (date) _____ . I will do my best to be organized, and I will report back to my class accurately and truthfully about how I used this skill and what the outcomes were.

_____   _____
Signed by student   Signed by teacher

LESSON 27. USING SELF-CONTROL

Review of Lesson 26 (Being Organized)

☞ **Important Points to Remember About Being Organized**

1. Keep track of your belongings.

2. Keep track of your appointments and other responsibilities.

3. Wear a watch.

4. Prioritize things you need to do.

Lesson 27. Using Self-Control

⊟ **Negative Example**

Narrator: Mr. James, an old friend of Jeff's dad, is visiting from the East Coast. All through dinner, Mr. James has been bragging about how wonderful the East is, what great weather it has, the interesting things to do there, etc.

Mr. James: Well, Jeff, what do you do for excitement around here?

Jeff: Well, gosh, Mr. James, mostly on Saturdays I just go out to the fields and watch the corn grow. My friends and I used to hang out at the fire station and wait for a call to come in so we could watch the truck go out, but since they put in the stop light on Main Street we just sit down there and watch it change color.

Dad: I think that's Jeff's idea of being funny. You may go to your room and study, Jeff. I'll speak to you later.

Jeff: Dad, you said I could go roller-skating tonight.

Dad: That was before you became such a comedian. I'll see you in your room later.

⊞ **Positive Example**

Mr. James: Well, Jeff, what do you do for excitement around here?

Jeff: Well, I'm on the soccer team and I play video games a lot with my friends.

Mr. James: I'm not too familiar with video games. I'd like to try some.

Jeff: If you like I could show you how to play some tomorrow. Right now I have some studying to do so I can meet my friends at the skating rink. Dad, may I be excused?

Mr. James: See you later, Jeff. (to Jeff's dad) What a nice kid. Very well mannered.

☞ **Important Points to Remember About Using Self-Control**

1. Think about the consequences before saying or doing anything.

2. Use self-talk.

3. If you need to, leave the situation as soon as possible.

4. Reward yourself for being successful.

EXERCISE 1

Narrator: Ernie is cleaning out the garage. He's hot and miserable. He thinks to himself: "What would happen if I just quit doing this and went swimming right now? The garage would be in a worse mess than when I started, because all this stuff is all over the driveway and Mom can't even get the car in now. No, I'm going to finish cleaning it out. It should only take about a half hour to get all this stuff organized. Then this afternoon when I do go to the pool I'm gonna spend some of that money I'll earn for cleaning the garage on a huge milkshake."

✔ **Checklist For Exercise 1**

Did Ernie . . .	Yes	No
1. Think about the consequences before leaving his work?	☐	☐
2. Use self-talk?	☐	☐
3. Leave the situation as soon as possible if necessary?	☐	☐
4. Reward himself for being successful?	☐	☐

EXERCISE 2

Narrator: Jill's doctor gave her a diet to follow so she could overcome a weight problem. Jill is at a movie with friends and is tempted to have some candy and ice cream. She thinks to herself: "I'd really like just one ice cream bar. But if I do that I might think, 'Well, I'm off my diet anyway, I might as well really go off it and have a lot of junk.' Besides, I've worked too hard on this diet to blow it now. (walking away from the candy counter) I'm not going to eat anything, and when I go get weighed tomorrow I'll really be proud. I'm starting to look better, too, everybody says so. I think I'll go check out some clothing sales tomorrow and see if I can wear a size 10 yet."

✔ Checklist For Exercise 2

Did Jill . . .

	Yes	No
1. Think about the consequences before eating ice cream and candy?	☐	☐
2. Use self-talk?	☐	☐
3. Leave the situation as soon as possible if necessary?	☐	☐
4. Reward herself?	☐	☐

EXERCISE 3

Narrator: Andy has been saving money for his Spanish class's trip to Mexico in the spring. If he doesn't save $400, he can't go. He's in a record store at the local mall with his friend Jack and sees a new album by his favorite group. He just got his allowance and has more than enough money with him to buy the album.

Andy: Man, I've been waiting for this album to come out for months! I hear it's great.

Jack: Me, too. Why don't you get it?

Andy: I can't. I only have two months to save $100 more or I can't go to Mexico.

Jack: Two months! That's a long time. You'll have plenty of money by then. Why don't you go think about it while we look around a little more?

Andy: Well, OK.

Narrator: Five minutes later.

Andy: I'm going to get that album. I'm sick of saving all the time and never being able to buy anything.

Jack: Way to go! Can I borrow it sometime?

✔ Checklist For Exercise 3

Did Andy . . .

	Yes	No
1. Think about the consequences before buying the album?	☐	☐
2. Use self-talk?	☐	☐
3. Get out of the situation as soon as possible if necessary?	☐	☐
4. Reward himself for being successful?	☐	☐

★ Situational Role Play Evaluation Guidelines

	Situational Role Play				
	#1	#2	#3	#4	#5
1. Think about the consequences before saying or doing anything.	—	—	—	—	—
2. Use self-talk.	—	—	—	—	—
3. If you need to, leave the situation as soon as possible.	—	—	—	—	—
4. Reward yourself for being successful.	—	—	—	—	—
Apply the Triple A Strategy	—	—	—	—	—

Lesson 27
Student Contract

Directions: Fill in the blanks with the appropriate answers and check with your teacher.

In what situation will you use the skill of using self-control?

_____

_____

_____

What do you think might happen if you don't use this skill in this situation?

_____

_____

_____

What people will be most affected when you use this skill?

_____

_____

_____

What do you expect to happen when you use this skill?

_____

_____

_____

I agree to try this skill with all its important points the next time I am faced with a situation that requires self-control. I will do my best to use self-control, and I will report back to my class accurately and truthfully about how I used the skill and what the outcomes were.

_____   _____
Signed by student   Signed by teacher

LESSON 28. DOING WHAT YOU AGREE TO DO

Review of Lesson 27 (Using Self-Control)

☞ **Important Points to Remember About Using Self-Control**

1. Think about the consequences before saying or doing anything.

2. Use self-talk.

3. If you need to, leave the situation as soon as possible.

4. Reward yourself for being successful.

Lesson 28. Doing What You Agree to Do

⊟ **Negative Example**

Narrator: Tom, Annie, and Sarah are on the Spring Dance Committee, finishing their final meeting before tomorrow's dance.

Tom: I need everyone to be here to decorate at 2:00 p.m. sharp. Any problems with that, can everybody be here?

Sarah: I can!

Annie: Uh, sure, whatever . . .

Tom: Who can I count on to call the band to make sure they are all here?

Annie: Oh, I'll take care of that.

Tom: If there are any problems or questions or if anybody needs help – please call me tonight. I'll be home.

Narrator: Next day they are setting up for the dance.

Sarah: Hey, Tom, we sure could use Annie's help getting some of this stuff up. *Where* is she??? It's already 2:20!

Tom: I have no idea. She said she'd be here just like everyone else. I'm getting worried about the band. They aren't here yet either! I told her to call me if there was any problem.

Sarah: You mean she didn't even call? Now I'm worried, too. Why didn't we just take care of it ourselves?

Annie: (enters gym) Hi guys, sorry I'm late. I forgot until just now. Anyway, I had something else to do.

Tom: (angry) Looks like we're not the only thing you forgot! Where's the band, Annie? You were supposed to call them, remember?! Everyone will be arriving in just a few minutes.

Annie: Oh no! The band! I lost their phone number and forgot to call you!

Sarah: Oh, that's just great, Annie. Now we'll all look like a bunch of jerks. Some dance with no band, thanks to you. (walks off upset)

⊞ **Positive Example**

Tom: I need everyone to be here at 2:00 p.m. to set up. Any problems?

Annie: I want to help but I know I can't be here until at least 2:20 because I have to post Monday's assembly schedule first.

Tom: That's fine as long as I know I can get someone to cover for you until then. Who will agree to contact the band?

Annie: I'll do it, but I think I need their phone number. I'll call you.

Narrator: Later that evening . . .

Annie: Tom, I just thought I'd let you know I saw the band in the gym practicing. I told them all to be setting up by 2:00.

Tom: Perfect. Thanks for calling and letting me know. I sure hope you'll be on the dance committee next time, Annie.

☞ **Important Points to Remember About Doing What You Agree To Do**

1. Check your schedule and other commitments.

2. Do not make a commitment you cannot keep.

3. Follow through on the agreement.

4. Keep others informed.

EXERCISE 1

Narrator: Mary has made arrangements with her teacher, Mr. Sherman, to meet right after school for some help on an assignment. As she approaches Mr. Sherman's room, Coach stops her in the hall.

Coach: Mary! You're just who I need to see. We have a team member who's absent. Can you substitute in the game today?

Mary: Uh, sure, I guess, when?

Coach: You need to be suited up in 20 minutes.

Narrator: Thirty minutes later

Coach: We're waiting for Mary, anybody seen her?

Team member: Mary? Count her out. I just saw her in Mr. Sherman's room. She's not even dressed yet.

Coach: We don't have enough to play. I guess we will just have to forfeit the game.

✔ Checklist For Exercise 1

Did Mary . . .

	Yes	No
1. Check her schedule and other commitments?	☐	☐
2. Not make (avoid making) a commitment she could not keep?	☐	☐
3. Follow through on the agreement?	☐	☐
4. Keep others informed?	☐	☐

EXERCISE 2

Kim: Jerry, there you are! You agreed to make my campaign posters and put them up. I don't see one of them. Everyone else's have been up for a week.

Jerry: I'm sorry, Kim. I didn't plan on being sick the last two days. I do have them all made like I said I would.

Kim: Jerry, what good are they if they aren't up? I'm sorry you were sick, but couldn't you have at least called someone to pick them up or got a message to me somehow?

Jerry: I didn't think it was that big of a deal.

Kim: You wouldn't, Jerry. You are not the one who is losing this election!

✔ Checklist For Exercise 2

Did Jerry . . .

	Yes	No
1. Check his schedule and other commitments?	☐	☐

	Yes	No
2. Not make (avoid making) a commitment he could not keep?	☐	☐
3. Follow through on the agreement?	☐	☐
4. Keep others informed?	☐	☐

EXERCISE 3

Cindy: Hi, Mrs. Nelson, I said I'd get back to you today about that baby-sitting job in the afternoons.

Mrs. Nelson: Yes, you did, thank you for calling me back. I didn't want to worry about it for one more day. What did you decide?

Cindy: Well, I worked out my schedule. I can work from 3:30 to 5:30 Monday through Thursday. On Fridays, I have pep club.

Mrs. Nelson: Couldn't you stay until 6:00?

Cindy: No, I've already checked, I need to be home by then. Also, you need to know that I'm only saying yes for this semester, because I don't know what my schedule will be next term.

Several weeks later . . .

Mrs. Nelson: Hello to our favorite baby sitter, you're always right on time.

Cindy: Thanks, Mrs. Nelson, this job has really helped me out.

Mrs. Nelson: Well, you deserve a job, Cindy. You've been very dependable and I know I can always count on you.

✔ Checklist For Exercise 3

Did Cindy . . .

	Yes	No
1. Check her schedule and other commitments?	☐	☐
2. Not make (avoid making) a commitment she couldn't keep?	☐	☐
3. Follow through on the agreement?	☐	☐
4. Keep others informed?	☐	☐

★ **Situational Role Play Evaluation Guidelines**

	Situational Role Play				
	#1	**#2**	**#3**	**#4**	**#5**
1. Check your schedule and other commitments.	—	—	—	—	—
2. Do not make a commitment you cannot keep.	—	—	—	—	—
3. Follow through on the agreement.	—	—	—	—	—
4. Keep others informed.	—	—	—	—	—
Apply the Triple A Strategy	—	—	—	—	—

Lesson 28
Student Contract

Directions: This report form should be completed the next time you make an agreement. Please fill it out and report back to your teacher about the outcomes.

In what situation did you use the skill of doing what you agree to do?

_____

_____

_____

What people were affected by your agreement?

_____

_____

_____

What happened when you used this skill?

_____

_____

_____

What might have happened if you hadn't used this skill?

_____

_____

_____

I agree to try to use the skill of doing what I agree to do with all its important points by (date) _____ . I will do my best to do the things I agree to do, and will report to my class accurately and truthfully about how I used this skill and what the outcomes were.

_____   _____
Signed by student   Signed by teacher

LESSON 29. ACCEPTING THE CONSEQUENCES OF YOUR ACTIONS

Review of Lesson 28 (Doing What You Agree to Do)

☞ **Important Points to Remember About Doing What You Agree to Do**

1. Check your schedule and other commitments.

2. Do not make a commitment you cannot keep.

3. Follow through on the agreement.

4. Keep others informed.

Lesson 29. Accepting the Consequences of Your Actions

⊟ **Negative Example**

Narrator: Jesse tried to sneak into the school dance without paying. Mr. Sims, the principal, caught him.

Mr. Sims: Jesse, could I see your ticket, please?

Jesse: Oh, I guess I lost it.

Mr. Sims: Did you get a stamp on your hand?

Jesse: Uh . . .

Mr. Sims: You didn't pay the admission charge, did you Jesse?

Jesse: Hey, it's Eric's fault! He dared me to do it. If you kick me out, kick him out too.

Mr. Sims: You don't have to leave, Jesse, just go back and pay the admission price.

Jesse: I didn't do anything wrong. I'm leaving. This place is dead anyway.

⊞ **Positive Example**

Mr. Sims: May I see your ticket, Jesse?

Jesse: Oh, hi, Mr. Sims. Guess you caught me.

Mr. Sims: You didn't buy a ticket, did you?

Jesse: No, I'm sorry. I thought I'd see if I could get away with it. Pretty dumb, huh? Can I go back and buy a ticket, do you want me to leave or what?

Mr. Sims: Just go get in the ticket line and don't try it again, OK?

Jesse: Don't worry. Thanks! (to himself) Well, that wasn't the smartest thing I ever did, but at least I didn't make it worse by lying about it or arguing with Mr. Sims. I sure won't do something like that again.

☞ **Important Points to Remember About Accepting the Consequences of Your Actions**

1. Admit your mistakes; don't make excuses.

2. Apologize.

3. Find out the consequences and accept them.

4. Think about how to avoid repeating your mistakes.

5. Get beyond your mistakes.

EXERCISE 1

Narrator: Leann was baby-sitting for a neighbor when she broke a glass.

Leann: Mrs. Larson, I'm so sorry, I dropped glass in the sink and it broke. I'd be glad to pay for it out of my earnings. If you'll tell me where you got it I'll replace it.

Mrs. Larson: Oh, Leann, don't worry about it. It wasn't anything special. Thanks for telling me about it. It looks like you really cleaned up the sink well.

Leann: (leaves and thinks to herself) Boy, what a klutz! I'm so clumsy. I can't believe a nice lady like that wants me for a baby sitter. Next time I'll probably burn the house down.

✔ **Checklist For Exercise 1**

Did Leann . . .	Yes	No
1. Admit her mistake, not make excuses?	☐	☐
2. Apologize?	☐	☐
3. Find out the consequences and accept them?	☐	☐
4. Think about how to avoid repeating her mistake?	☐	☐

5. Get beyond her mistake? ☐ ☐

EXERCISE 2

Narrator: Ted is watching TV when his sister Janet rushes in.

Janet: How could you do that to me?

Ted: Do what?

Janet: Embarrass me in front of my friends like you did just now.

Ted: (laughing) You mean when I told them about the time you threw up all over the back seat of the car? So what?

Janet: I almost died of embarrassment and you're just laughing about it.

Ted: You're too sensitive. I'm here to teach you humility, Sis.

Janet: (leaves in tears) *You* are insensitive!

✔ Checklist For Exercise 2

Did Ted . . .   **Yes   No**

1. Admit his mistake, not make excuses?   ☐ ☐

2. Apologize?   ☐ ☐

3. Find out the consequences and accept them?   ☐ ☐

4. Think about how to avoid repeating his mistake?   ☐ ☐

5. Get beyond his mistake?   ☐ ☐

EXERCISE 3

Narrator: Carrie joins her family at the breakfast table.

Dad: You got in pretty late last night, Carrie.

Carrie: I know, I'm sorry, Dad. It won't happen again. I just lost track of time because I was having fun.

Dad: You know what your curfew is.

Carrie: Right. And I won't be out past curfew again ever, I promise.

Dad: A deal is a deal, Carrie. You know what happens when you don't keep your part of the bargain.

Carrie: You're not going to ground me are you? You can't! I've got plans tonight. I said I was sorry. What else do you want me to do?

Dad: I want you to learn to keep your part of the deal and accept the consequences when you don't.

Carrie: Oh great. Now I get a lecture, too.

✔ Checklist For Exercise 3

Did Carrie . . .   **Yes   No**

1. Admit her mistake, not make excuses?   ☐ ☐

2. Apologize?   ☐ ☐

3. Find out the consequences and accept them?   ☐ ☐

4. Think about how to avoid repeating her mistake?   ☐ ☐

5. Get beyond her mistake?   ☐ ☐

★ Situational Role Play Evaluation Guidelines

| | **Situational Role Play** | | | | |
	#1	**#2**	**#3**	**#4**	**#5**
1. Admit your mistakes; don't make excuses.	—	—	—	—	—
2. Apologize.	—	—	—	—	—
3 Find out the consequences and accept them.	—	—	—	—	—
4. Think about how to avoid repeating your mistakes.	—	—	—	—	—
5. Get beyond your mistakes.	—	—	—	—	—
Apply the Triple A Strategy	—	—	—	—	—

Lesson 29
Student Contract

Directions: Since no one knows when you will need to accept the consequences of a mistake, we can't write a contract to use this skill by a certain date. Instead, here is a report form to use the next time you need to accept the consequences of your actions. Fill it out and report back to your teacher about the outcomes.

In what situation did you use the skill of accepting the consequences of your actions?

_____

_____

_____

What people were involved when you used the skill?

_____

_____

_____

What happened when you used this skill?

_____

_____

_____

What might have happened if you hadn't used this skill?

_____

_____

_____

I agree to try this skill the next time I make a mistake and need to accept the consequences of that mistake. I will report back to my class or teacher truthfully and accurately about how I used the skill and what the outcomes were.

_____   _____
Signed by student   Signed by teacher

LESSON 30. COPING WITH BEING UPSET OR DEPRESSED

Review of Lesson 29 (Accepting the Consequences of Your Actions)

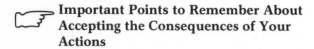 **Important Points to Remember About Accepting the Consequences of Your Actions**

1. Admit your mistakes; don't make excuses.

2. Apologize.

3. Find out the consequences and accept them.

4. Think about how to avoid repeating your mistakes.

5. Get beyond your mistakes.

Lesson 30. Coping with Being Upset or Depressed

 **Negative Example**

Narrator: David and Holly have just failed a test that neither studied for. Upset, they join a group of their friends between classes.

Holly: (loudly) HI GUYS, did anybody else FAIL that TEST, TOO? HA, HA, HA. Like we didn't EVEN READ the QUESTIONS; WE JUST GAVE IT UP!

David: Holly, do you have to use a loudspeaker to advertise everything? I feel absolutely sick!

Group Member A: Yeah, easy Holly; it was a midterm, you know. I wouldn't say it's the end of the world though, David.

David: (looking very upset) It *is* the end of the world! I don't think I'll be able to make the team next semester! My parents will never understand – they'll kill me!

Group Member B: Oh, poor David, you make me want to cry. You're not the only one who ever had to take a semester off from the team, you know. I . . .

Holly: (interrupting) DON'T BE SO SERIOUS. DON'T WORRY ABOUT ANYTHING! Speaking of the team – how's your GRUESOME knee?

David: Wait 'til you guys see this (shows knee injury). I'll never be the same. It's killing me. I also scraped my back and lost my mitt. Some game. I'm so bummed.

Group Member A: Do us a favor, David, *don't* show us your back, too. What do you say we get off this party line, guys, and dial into what's going on over there. (points to another group of people)

Group Member B: I'm with you. You two deserve each other. Holly Hyper meets Dave Depressed.

 **Positive Example**

Group Member A: How are you, Holly?

Holly: Oh, a little ragged after that test. I didn't study enough. I'm pretty keyed up; I think I'll go get a drink of water, take some deep breaths, and try to calm down. Then David and I will have to go study, so this doesn't happen again.

David: Right, we really slacked off. Not the best move for a midterm. Did you guys study a lot?

Group Member B: A ton; it was a biggy.

David: I think I'm going to have to quit playing ball and start playing library. You took a semester off the team, didn't you? What did you tell your parents?

Group Member B: Yeah, I did. I told them that playing ball was really interfering with studying because I was so tired all the time. They really understood. You'd be surprised. Hey, how's your knee, anyway?

David: It looks bad but it feels a lot better today. You see me walkin', don't you ? Watch this – ankle express!

Group Members: (laugh)

David: Besides, you guys were great out there.

Holly: (re-enters group) Well, David, shall we? It's free period; let's not waste any time. We're studying for this one!

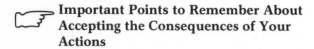 **Important Points to Remember About Coping With Being Upset or Depressed**

1. Recognize your feelings.

2. Identify the cause of your feelings.

3. Avoid "horriblizing," especially to others.

4. Take productive action.

EXERCISE 1

Narrator: Sally and Nancy are two overweight girls attending a school dance.

Nancy: Hi, Sally, I'm so glad you're here! I was feeling a little nervous about finally coming to a school dance after avoiding them for so long.

Sally: I'm so depressed! I told you nobody would ask us to dance! Let's just go home and make hot fudge cake, huh?

Nancy: Come on, Sally, we agreed to try this time, remember?

Sally: Who are you kidding? No one will dance with the two pigarinas!

Nancy: Wait a minute, we've both worked really hard to start losing; we're five pounds less already. I'm proud of that. Besides, I'd like to concentrate on how nice we look tonight.

Sally: Nice compared to what? Twin tanks? Why bother? Let's just go get some refreshments. That's where we belong anyway.

Nancy: No, Sally. Let's go over and ask someone to dance. It'll get your mind off food.

Sally: Give it up! What are you gonna do when Mr. Someone says no?

Nancy: Well, I won't die, that's for sure. Besides, maybe some of the guys in our conditioning class are just as self-conscious. I'm gonna go ask Phil; he's looking over here.

Sally: Well, feel free – I'm going to the refreshment table.

Narrator: Nancy and Phil move on to the dance floor as Sally eats cookies and watches miserably.

✔ Checklist A For Exercise 1

Did Sally . . .   Yes   No

1. Recognize her feelings?   ☐   ☐

2. Identify the cause of her feelings?   ☐   ☐

3. Avoid horriblizing, especially to others?   ☐   ☐

4. Take productive action?   ☐   ☐

✔ Checklist B For Exercise 1

Did Nancy . . .   Yes   No

1. Recognize her feelings?   ☐   ☐

2. Identify the cause of her feelings?   ☐   ☐

3. Avoid horriblizing, especially to others?   ☐   ☐

4. Take productive action?   ☐   ☐

EXERCISE 2

Narrator: Billy and Shirley have met up with each other at the track unexpectedly after school. All of their friends are at the game.

Billy: Hey, Shirley, you look as bummed as I do. What are you doing here when everyone else is having fun at the game?

Shirley: Same thing as you are, I guess, trying to run off what's bothering us?

Billy: Yeah, why ruin everyone else's fun? Wanna talk about it?

Shirley: Yeah, sure. The tension is pretty tight at home. My dad just got laid off and I'm pretty sure my brother is moving out.

Billy: I think I might know how you feel. My parents are talking divorce again these days . . .

Shirley: You know, Billy, running really helps me; but I think we should go talk to the counselor. We need more help than exercise can give us.

Billy: Well, I hadn't really thought of discussing my feelings with anybody.

Shirley: You just told me, didn't you? It wasn't so bad, was it?

Billy: No, but you're a friend. What can a counselor do?

Shirley: Give us suggestions; help us understand what's happening. Let's make an appointment together. We can support each other in this, OK?

Billy: You're right, let's do it right now. I'm glad we talked.

✔ Checklist For Exercise 2

Did Shirley and Billy . . .   Yes   No

1. Recognize their feelings?   ☐   ☐

2. Identify the cause of their feelings?   ☐   ☐

3. Avoid horriblizing, especially to others?   ☐   ☐

4. Take productive action?   ☐   ☐

EXERCISE 3

Richie: Hey, Marsha, how's it going? That's some lunch you got there, only an apple?

Marsha: Not too hungry today, I guess. Guess I've been down in the dumps and I finally figured out what's bugging me.

Richie: Well, what is it?

Marsha: I'm jealous.

Richie: Well, at least you can admit it to yourself, that's pretty good. Jealous of whom?

Marsha: (dramatically pointing to a nearby group) Jealous of that THING! That new girl who is just goo-gooing over Tom Martin! She makes me sick!

Richie: Easy, Marsha. She's really pretty nice. She actually did a lot of work on our group project, remember?

Marsha: Yeah, I remember all right. She and Tom Martin did a lot of work. I personally can't stand her! Now look at her, she's whispering to him. Let's throw something over there and see what she does.

Richie: Get off it, Marsha, when are you gonna grow up? Anyway, I don't want to eat your problems for lunch – I'm outta here.

✔ Checklist For Exercise 3

Did Marsha . . .   Yes   No

1. Recognize her feelings?   ☐   ☐

2. Identify the cause of her feelings?   ☐   ☐

3. Avoid horriblizing, especially to others?   ☐   ☐

4. Take productive action?   ☐   ☐

★ Situational Role Play Evaluation Guidelines

	Situational Role Play				
	#1	#2	#3	#4	#5
1. Recognize your feelings.	—	—	—	—	—
2. Identify the cause of your feelings.	—	—	—	—	—
3. Avoid horriblizing, especially to others.	—	—	—	—	—
4. Take productive action.	—	—	—	—	—
Apply the Triple A Strategy	—	—	—	—	—

Lesson 30
Student Contract

Directions: This report form should be completed the next time you are faced with an upsetting situation or feelings. Please fill it out and report back to your teacher about the outcomes.

In what situation did you use the skill of coping with being upset or depressed?

_____

_____

Were other people involved when you used this skill? If so, how?

_____

_____

What might have happened if you hadn't used this skill in this situation?

_____

_____

What happened when you used the skill of coping with being upset or depressed?

_____

_____

Have your situation or feelings improved in any way since you used this skill?

_____

_____

If you need more help in this situation or with these feelings, how might you get it or who can you meet with for assistance?

_____

_____

I agree to use the skill of coping with being upset or depressed the next time I am faced with an upsetting incident or feelings. I will do my best to cope effectively with being upset or depressed and will report back to (class or teacher) about how I used this skill and what the outcomes were.

_____   _____
Signed by student   Signed by teacher

LESSON 31. FEELING GOOD ABOUT YOURSELF

Review of Lesson 30 (Coping with Being Upset or Depressed)

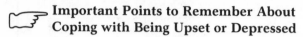 **Important Points to Remember About Coping with Being Upset or Depressed**

1. Recognize your feelings.

2. Identify the cause of your feelings.

3. Avoid horriblizing, especially to others.

4. Take productive action.

Lesson 31. Feeling Good About Yourself

⊟ Negative Example

Narrator: Carla has never put much effort into studying. She has a habit of procrastinating and then is disappointed when she doesn't do well. Many times she counts on her friend, Lisa, to help her with school work and to get by. Carla is sure that Lisa has been avoiding her lately. Today they are taking one of their competency tests. Carla is tired, having stayed up most of the night cramming and watching videos on television.

Lisa: Hey, Carla, are you all set for this?

Carla: Sure, I studied. Where have you been lately? Why haven't you called me?

Lisa: I got a job at the library. I've been studying there when it's slow. I've also been spending some time with Seth.

Carla: You could've called to tell me. So much for friendship, now I'll never pass this test!

Lisa: I thought you said you studied? Besides, you could call me too, you know. Don't get upset about it now. You'll never pass with that attitude!

Carla: I'm not upset!

Narrator: Nervous, tired, and angry with Lisa, Carla can't concentrate during the exam. When Lisa gets up to sharpen her pencil, Carla cannot resist the chance to copy Lisa's answers.

Lisa: (returns to desk and whispers) Carla, what do you think you're doing?

Carla: Shut up, Lisa! We'll get in trouble.

Mrs. Tucker: Carla, bring your test up to my desk right away, please.

Carla: (scowls at Lisa) Thanks a lot!

Mrs. Tucker: Do you think you are prepared to take this test today?

Carla: Of course I am.

Mrs. Tucker: Why is it you feel that you have to copy Lisa's paper then?

Carla: Are you accusing me of cheating?

Mrs. Tucker: I'm not asking you, I watched you; I know you cheated. But I'm trying to understand why. You know you have several opportunities to take this test this year.

Carla: I wasn't cheating! Besides, I could care less about this stupid test anyway. Why should I care if I graduate? Why don't you just trash it?

Mrs. Tucker: I'm afraid you leave me no choice.

Carla: Fine!! (stomps off)

⊞ Positive Example

Narrator: Carla has been meeting regularly with Mrs. Tucker after school in order to get ready to take the competency test again. At this time they are finishing their last study session.

Mrs. Tucker: Well, Carla, I'm very pleased that you decided to come back and work things out. You should be proud of yourself for being able to do that; and for working so hard. How are you feeling about the test tomorrow?

Carla: Oh, a little nervous, but I think I have it under control. I keep telling myself I *can* do it – on my own this time!

Mrs. Tucker: It's good to hear you sound sure of yourself. I know it hasn't been easy.

Carla: No, I'm not a natural. I have had problems with putting things off. But I finally realized how much it means to me to pass this test myself. Since I'm not the smartest kid on the block, well, that means a lot of extra work on my part.

Mrs. Tucker: Right. I bet you feel a lot better about yourself. Cheating never got anybody anywhere. You've come a long way since we started and I'm sure you'll do well.

Carla: Thanks, Mrs. Tucker. I realize now that cheating hasn't helped me. You've changed my attitude about teachers. My goal this year is to *graduate*, right next to my friend Lisa.

Mrs. Tucker: Lisa Barrett? Are you two friends again?

Carla: Oh yes, I apologized. I told her I knew I wasn't being fair to her, putting her under that much pressure and all. We worked it out.

Mrs. Tucker: That's good. And good luck tomorrow. You're on your way to graduation, Carla!

👉 **Important Points to Remember About Feeling Good about Yourself**

1. Think positively.
2. Be honest with yourself.
3. Set standards for your behavior.
4. Set goals for yourself.
5. Resolve problems with others.

EXERCISE 1

Narrator: Clarissa is a sophomore on the junior varsity tennis team. Lately, she has slacked off at practice and has not had a very good season. Clarissa still feels she deserves to make the varsity tennis team next year. She's now at game point with Sophia, a junior competitor. The winner of the match will be the one selected for the varsity team. Once the ball is served, Clarissa sees it land on the line, but is unable to get into position for the return.

Clarissa: It was *out*! O-U-T, out!!!

Coach: No, Clarissa, it was in. The game's over. Sophia will play varsity next year.

Sophia: (approaches net) Come on, Clarissa, let's shake on it. It was a tight game. (extending her hand)

Clarissa: (angrily throws down her racket) Yeah, that's easy for you to say – how could you do this to me?

Coach: Don't you think you're setting a poor example for sportsmanship on this team? I think if you work on your game *and* your attitude next year, you'll still have a good chance to play varsity.

Clarissa: You both had it in for me! I won't make the team. I hate tennis. I quit! For good!

✔ **Checklist For Exercise 1**

Did Clarissa . . .	Yes	No
1. Think positively?	☐	☐
2. Be honest with herself?	☐	☐
3. Set standards for her behavior?	☐	☐
4. Set goals for herself?	☐	☐
5. Resolve problems with others?	☐	☐

EXERCISE 2

Narrator: Diana and Freddie have been dating each other regularly for 4 months. After school, they meet to discuss their plans for Friday night. Their discussion turns into an argument and both of them end up leaving. Having thought about what happened on the way home, Diana decides to call Freddie.

Diana: Hi, Freddie, it's me. Listen, we have a good relationship going here. I know that. So I think we can work this whole thing out. OK?

Freddie: But you told me you would go to Alex's party with me on Friday and now you just refuse!

Diana: It's not that I don't want to go to the party with you. It's just that I don't like being around all those rowdies. I don't fit in that crowd, I'm not like them, and I don't want to be.

Freddie: OK, so I understand now – Why didn't you say so before?

Diana: Because I thought you would think it was a stupid reason. On the way home I realized that if you knew how I felt about it, you'd probably understand.

Freddie: Okay, so what's one party, anyway? Sorry I left in a huff, I'm glad you called.

Diana: I'm sorry too. I have to work on communicating better in the first place instead of getting so upset like I did this afternoon.

Freddie: Now that's something we can work on together.

✔ Checklist For Exercise 2

Did Diana . . .   **Yes** **No**

1. Think positively?   ☐   ☐

2. Be honest with herself?   ☐   ☐

3. Set standards for her behavior?   ☐   ☐

4. Set goals for herself?   ☐   ☐

5. Resolve problems with others?   ☐   ☐

EXERCISE 3

Narrator: Corey is being interviewed for a job at a bicycle shop.

Interviewer: Corey, why do you think you're the person for this job?

Corey: Because I want to learn more about bicycle repairs. It's always been a hobby of mine and I work hardest at things I like doing.

Interviewer: Do you not work as hard on things you don't like?

Corey: To be honest, no. But I think you like what you're good at. I've always been best doing things with my hands.

Interviewer: What can I expect of you as a worker on the floor?

Corey: Well, I think you have to cater to customers but at the same time be reasonable. That is, listen to what they want, give them information, be as helpful as you can, and be able to work out problems.

Interviewer: What are some of your personal goals that working here might help you accomplish?

Corey: Someday I'd like to work on the racing circuit doing repairs on all kinds of bikes. That means I need to learn about, and get experience with, working on different makes and models. It also means I'll need to work on speed and accuracy.

Interviewer: What do you think makes a good employee besides technical skills?

Corey: I'd say honesty is the most important thing. But also things like not wasting time at work, being prompt, sticking to your assigned schedule, being able to get along with other employees.

Interviewer: I can tell from your answers that you are someone who feels pretty good about yourself. So when can you start? You just got yourself a job.

✔ Checklist For Exercise 3

Did Corey seem like someone who . . .   **Yes** **No**

1. Thinks positively?   ☐   ☐

2. Is honest with himself?   ☐   ☐

3. Sets standards for his behavior?   ☐   ☐

4. Sets goals for himself?   ☐   ☐

5. Resolves problems with others?   ☐   ☐

★ Situational Role Play Evaluation Guidelines

	Situational Role Play				
	#1	**#2**	**#3**	**#4**	**#5**
1. Think positively.	—	—	—	—	—
2. Be honest with yourself.	—	—	—	—	—
3. Set standards for your behavior.	—	—	—	—	—
4. Set goals for yourself.	—	—	—	—	—
5. Resolve problems with others.	—	—	—	—	—
Apply the Triple A Strategy	—	—	—	—	—

Lesson 31
Student Contract

Directions: Fill in the blanks with appropriate answers and check with your teacher.

In what situation(s) will you use the skill of feeling good about yourself?

_____

_____

_____

How will you use the important points of this skill in the situation(s) you have described above?

_____

_____

_____

What do you expect will happen if you use the skill of feeling good about yourself as you have described above?

_____

_____

_____

What might happen if you didn't use the skill of feeling good about yourself in the situation(s) you described above?

_____

_____

_____

I agree to try to use the skill of feeling good about myself with all of its important points by (date) _____ . I will do my best to feel good about myself and will report back to my class accurately and truthfully about how I used this skill.

_____   _____
Signed by student   Signed by teacher